Vedic Astrology

Series - 2

Stock Market Analysis

Jyotish Vachaspathi R.G. Krishnan

Published by
The Institute of Vedic Astrology
3813, Brantford Dr. Richardson, TX 75082
(972) 783-1242

ISBN 0-9715104-0-7

Disclaimer

The principles of Vedic Astrology discussed in this book are meant to be used as guidelines in arriving at proper conclusions regarding stock market trends. While applying these principles to delineate the market trends, it may be borne in mind that there is no guarantee that these principles will always give correct results.

TABLE OF CONTENTS

Om Gam Ganapathaye Namaha.

Vedic Astrology
Series-2

Stock Market Analysis

By Jyotish Vachaspathi R.G. Krishnan

Invocation Prayers

Ganapathi Gayathri

TAT PURUSHAAYA VIDHMAHEY
MAHA DEVAAYA DHEEMAHI
TANNO DHANTI PRACHODAYAT

I know that Purusha.
On that Maha Deva(Great Lord), I meditate.
May He inspire me.

Subrahmanya Gayathri

TAT PURUSHAAYA VIDHMAHEY
MAHASENAAYA DHEEMAHI
TANNA SHANMUKHA PRACHODAYAT

I know that Purusha.
On that Great Warrior God I meditate.
May the six faced God inspire me.

Dedication

This book is dedicated to:

My (late) parents, who were a source of great strength to me always from day one of my life until their last breath.

My First Guru in Vedic Astrology, (late) **Mr. Raja Iyer,** who when I was just a school kid, had kindled deep interest in my mind on the subject of Vedic Astrology. His accurate predictions given to various clients in my presence had made a deep impression in my mind about the greatness of Vedic Astrology.

My Spiritual Guru, 'Atmavidya Bhushanam', Sastra Ratnakara', 'Vidya Varidhi', Brahmashree, (late) Jagadeeswara Sastrigal of Madras, with whose blessings and initiation I could make good progress in the spiritual path of worship of Divine Mother and also in the field of Vedic Astrology.

My Living Guru, respected **Mr. C.S. Patel,** veteran Vedic Astrologer of Mumbai, winner of several titles and awards, who had taught me some intricate points concerning stock market astrology.

My loving wife, who has been a source of my inspiration always, at every stage of this book.

Appreciation

The author expresses his heartfelt appreciation to:

1) **Mr. Swanandesh Karandikar,** architect cum software engineer for all valuable assistance rendered by him and for his input regarding the stock market information.

2) **Mr. Ronald Carlson,** an executive, who is involved in the stock market on a day to day basis for his valuable assistance in regard to stock market information.

3) **Dr. Ronald Stewart,** for helping me with the past data regarding the stock markets.

4) **Mr. Balakumar** one of my very good well wishers for agreeing to get this book printed at his facility at Plano, TX.

Foreword

It gives me great pleasure to write this foreword to my disciple's book on “Stock Market Analysis”.

I have known Mr. Krishnan since 1982 when I first met him at an Astrological convention at Ahmedabad, India. Thereafter, we developed a good, teacher-student relationship and I was very happy to teach him the intricacies of Ashtaka Varga system of prediction and other advanced astrological techniques culled from various astrological classics and Nadi Granthas.

In my own younger days I had also dabbled in the stock markets using astrology and made much money. I have also taught Mr. Krishnan some interesting principles regarding stock market predictions. I am glad to learn that he had actually applied these principles to the New York Stock Exchange and has made several points in this book which are adequately supported by DJIA numbers.

I wish Mr. Krishnan all success and I am very sure that this book will receive a positive response from the astrology knowing readers who are also interested in the stock markets.

I trust that the intelligent readers of this book will succeed in their efforts in the stock markets by making judicial use of the important points developed in this novel treatise.

7/7/2001 — Mumbai, India.
Mr. C.S.Patel

Preface

I have been dabbling in financial astrology for over 10 years now. This forms part of mundane astrology. There are several books in the market on financial astrology by eminent authors. These were a source of great inspiration to me for the last several years.

I have been writing since the year 1990 a column in **PALANI PANCHANG,** an Indian Almanac published in English every year from Fremont, C.A. by **Mr. Devendra Trivedi**. In this column, every year, I have been giving an advanced forecast of the **Stock Market Trends** that are likely for that particular year.

Many readers of the **PALANI PANCHANG** have got back to me from time to time over the phone or through e-mail, appreciating the accuracy of my predictions. Over the years, I have tried to improve my predictive techniques by daily observing the stock market and by doing my one man research trying to find the reasons, if I went wrong.

Due to the blessings of God and my Gurus, success rate in my advance forecast of the stock market has improved a lot over the years. At the request of many friends and well-wishers, I am writing this book on "**Stock Market Analysis**".

Down the road, God willing, I propose to write a book on **"Astrological Analysis on Commodity Markets"** and a little later, another book, on **"Astrological Analysis on Options Trading in the Stock Markets"** as desired by my well wishers.

R.G.Krishnan

Introduction

Napoleon Bonaparte is reported to have stated that greed and fear are the two levers which control mankind. Carl Jung, a famous psychologist has said, that "Astrology represents the summation of psychological knowledge of antiquity".

A famous investment advisor had stated, "Despite all computers and all fundamental technical analysis, the investor psychology is still the most significant factor in the stock market behavior".

Vedic Astrology seems to hold the key to understand investor psychology better and to arrive at proper conclusions about market trends. This is because the planets Moon and Mercury have a definite role to play in the psychology of individuals and also in mass psychology.

In Vedic Astrology, Moon is considered to control the mind of individuals and Mercury is considered to control the emotional as well as the nervous system of individuals. Thus, it is seen that the transiting positions of these planets have marked effects in the stock market trends when observed closely on a day-to-day basis.

What are the astrological factors which trigger such mass psychological reactions? One commonly noticed phenomenon is that whenever Mercury gets into retrogression mode there is a marked effect on mass psychology. Similarly, on lunation days, perceptible behavioral changes are noticed particularly in the case of lunatics. On lunation days there is perceptible effect on the tidal patterns and wave patterns in the oceans and seas.

Our human body is supposed to contain about 90% of fluid contents. If lunation can have an effect on the tidal patterns and wave patterns in the ocean, some subtle effects are also likely on the psychology of every human being, which in turn affect their behavioral patterns.

It has been statistically proved that whenever Mars and Saturn conjunct, there is a spurt in violent activities of human beings and there is a perceptible increase in crime rate. It is also noticed that eclipses, which occur on lunation days, affect the stock market and makes it either bullish or bearish.

Every layman who has no knowledge of astrology knows that every day is not the same in his behavioral pattern and on some days he feels low and on some days he feels high, the reason for which is not known to him. From these, it can be concluded that planetary movements do have an effect on mass psychology and as such, understanding the Vedic Astrology can help to understand stock market fluctuations with reference to planetary movements.

This book will be better understood by those who have some basic knowledge of astrology (Vedic Astrology or Western Astrology), as they will be able to effectively use the various techniques outlined in this book in their dealings on the stock market. Some conclusions are presented in this book about the trends in the stock markets that are likely in the year 2001 and 2002, with reasoning behind these conclusions. These reasoning are also meant for the laymen who have no basic knowledge of astrology but who are interested in knowing the stock market trends that are likely in these years. It is expected that these reasoning will motivate the lay reader to learn the Vedic Astrology and apply the principles brought out in this book for their own dealings in the Stock Market. For those conversant with the basics of astrology, the reasoning given is likely to enhance their ability to correctly pick the trends of the stock markets in future years. Currently, many Vedic Astrology software are available in the market which even a person with practically very little knowledge of astrology can make use of for getting astrological charts printed out of their P.C. and printers. Once the horoscope is generated, it will be easier to apply and understand the principles outlined herein. Laymen who find this book interesting should get themselves familiarized with the use

Of Ephemeris and also astrological software so that they can benefit without wasting their time on the preparation of charts.

The aim of the book is to help the reader to evaluate the long-term trends as well as short-term trends in the stock markets using the principles of Vedic Astrology. The methodology based on various planetary situations is discussed in the various chapters of this book. Every effort is made in this book to explain the points made by correlating the principles explained with the planetary situation at that point of time and with the corresponding DJIA numbers which ruled at that point of time. This will help the readers conversant with Vedic Astrology to understand the points more clearly.

Outer planets do have an effect on the stock market behavior pattern and as such they are also included in the discussion of the principles enumerated in this book.

For the benefit of laymen who may read this book, a Chapter has been included in which the basics of Vedic Astrology have been discussed. It is expected that many amongst them will get motivated to become more conversant with Vedic Astrology.

Chapter One

A) Basics of Vedic Astrology.

Zodiac

The Zodiac is a broad band in the heavens extending about 8^0 on either side of the ecliptic (Sun's path of apparent motion is called the ecliptic). The Zodiac consisting of 360 degrees is divided into 12 parts of 30^0. Each part is a sign, which are Aries, Taurus, Gemini, Cancer, Leo, Virgo, Libra, Scorpio, Sagittarius, Capricorn, Aquarius and Pisces.

Nine Planets: The classics of Vedic Astrology deal with only nine planets namely, Sun, Moon, Mars, Mercury, Jupiter, Venus, Saturn, Rahu and Ketu. In the Tropical Astrology as practiced in the West, the outer planets namely, Uranus, Neptune and Pluto are always taken into consideration.

It is also statistically proven that the outer planets have a bearing on the Stock Market trends. The Author, like many other Vedic Astrologers, also believes that the outer planets do have an impact on the Stock Market trends and as such the outer planets are also discussed in this book with reference to their impact on the Stock Markets.

Planetary Velocities: All the planets revolve in orbits around the Sun. Although the Earth revolves around the Sun, for the purpose of astrology we assume that the Sun goes around the Earth. This apparent path of the Sun is called the "Ecliptic". All the planets move at various speeds in their orbit.

Sun takes about 365 ¼ days for a complete revolution and it takes one month to transit each of the 12 zodiacal signs.

Moon is the fastest moving planet which goes around the Zodiac in 30 lunar days. Spending an average of 2 days and 12 hours in each of the 12 zodiacal signs.

Mars takes 18 months for a complete revolution and takes about 45 days to transit each of the 12 zodiacal signs.

Mercury takes about one year for a complete revolution and transits each of the 12 zodiacal signs at the rate of one month per Sign.

Jupiter takes 12 years for a complete revolution and transits each of the 12 zodiacal signs at the rate of one year per sign.

Venus takes about one year to complete the revolution and transits each of the 12 zodiacal signs at the rate of one month per Sign.

Saturn takes 30 yrs for a complete revolution and it transits each of the 12 zodiacal signs at the rate of 30 months per sign.

Rahu and **Ketu** take about 18 years for a complete revolution and transit each zodiacal sign at the rate of 18 months per sign.

Uranus was discovered in the year 1781 by Sir William Herschel. This planet takes about 84 years for a complete revolution and takes about 7 years to transit each of the 12 zodiacal signs.

Neptune is the third largest planet in the solar system and was discovered in 1846. This planet takes about 188 years to complete one revolution and about 14 years to transit each sign.

Pluto. This is the farthest most planet of the solar system and was discovered in the year 1930. This planet takes 252 years to complete one revolution and transits each of the 12 zodiacal signs at the rate of 21 years per sign.

All the planets except Rahu and Ketu move in a clockwise direction. Rahu and Ketu move anti-clockwise.

Planetary Ownership of the Zodiacal Signs

Aries and Scorpio are ruled by Mars. Taurus and Libra are ruled by Venus. Gemini and Virgo are ruled by Mercury. Cancer is ruled by the Moon. Leo is ruled by the Sun. Sagittarius and Pisces are ruled by Jupiter. Capricorn and Aquarius are both ruled by Saturn.

Combustion of Planets.

Planets become combust when they come within a certain distance from the Sun. This rule regarding combustion does not apply to Rahu and Ketu. On the other hand, they become more powerful while being close to Sun. Such periods are called "Eclipses". The Moon gets combust within 12 degrees on either side of the Sun. Mars gets combust within 17 degrees on either side of the Sun. Mercury gets combust within 14 degrees on either side of the Sun. Jupiter gets combust within 11 degrees on either side of the Sun. Venus gets combust within 10 degrees on either side of the Sun. Saturn gets combust within 15 degrees on either side of the Sun.

Acceleration of Planets.

The movement of a planet from one sign to another sometimes becomes more than the normal speed of the Planet concerned. In such cases, the concerned planet is said to be in acceleration.

Retrogression of Planets.

All planets except the Sun, Moon, Rahu and Ketu are subject to retrograde motion. The condition of retrogression is separate for the inner planets like Mercury and Venus and separate for the outer planets like Jupiter, Saturn, Rahu, Ketu, Uranus, Neptune and Pluto. In the case of the inner planets like Mercury and Venus, the retrogression commences after their inferior conjunction. As these planets move around their orbits, inferior conjunction occurs when these planets pass between the earth and Sun and superior conjunction occurs when these planets go behind the Sun. In the case of the outer planets, retrogression occurs when the planet in its apparent motion reaches a longitude before the opposition point. In the case of the outer planets, when they occupy the same longitude as the Sun, they are said to be in conjunction with the Sun. The planets are said to be in opposition with the Sun, when they occupy a longitude which is exactly 180^0 away from the Sun.

Naksahtras or Lunar Mansions. The entire zodiac is divided into 27 parts of 13^0 and 20' each. Each part is called a 'Nakshatra'. In Vedic Astrology, in dealing with the market forecasting, these Nakshatras play a vital part. The Nakshatras are further subdivided into four padas (or quarters). Thus, the entire zodiac will have 27 X 4= 108 padas. The 27 Nakshatras or the Lunar Mansions are shown below:

1) Aswini 2) Bharani 3) Krittika 4) Rohini 5) Mrigasira
6) Aridra 7) Punarvasu 8) Pushyami 9) Aslesha 10) Makha
11) Poorva Phalguni 12) Uttara Phalguni 13) Hasta
14) Chitra 15) Swati 16) Visakha 17) Anuradha
18) Jyeshta 19) Moola 20) Poorvashada 21) Uttarashada
22) Shravana 23) Dhanishta 24) Satabisha
25) Poorva Bhadra 26) Uttara Bhadra 27) Revathi.

Signs: The twelve signs mentioned above are classified into three groups namely Cardinal or Movable signs, Fixed signs and Common signs. They are:

Cardinal Signs: Aries, Cancer, Libra and Capricorn.
Fixed Signs: Taurus, Leo, Scorpio and Aquarius.
Common Signs: Gemini, Virgo, Sagittarius and Pisces.

These signs are again classified into Fiery, Earthy, Airy and Watery signs.

Fiery Signs: Aries, Leo and Sagittarius.
Earthy Signs: Taurus, Virgo and Capricorn.
Airy Signs: Gemini, Libra, and Aquarius.
Watery Signs: Cancer, Scorpio, and Pisces.

These are also divided into odd and even signs.

Odd Signs: Aries, Gemini, Leo, Libra, Sagittarius and Aquarius.

Even Signs: Taurus, Cancer, Virgo, Scorpio, Capricorn and Pisces.

Chart Format: In this book, the rectangular chart as used in the South India has been used to depict the planetary situation. Along with this, the longitudes of the planets in the sign where they are posited are given to enable the reader to understand the charts better. The basic chart is called the Rasi Chart. A typical Rasi Chart (rectangular Sidereal chart) may be seen at Chart # 1. For the laymen it is explained that this Chart is to be read in a clockwise manner. In this chart, the signs are fixed, but the ascendant will move to the sign concerned depending on the time of birth or the time of events etc. From this Rasi chart is derived the various Divisional Charts. The most important among the divisional charts is the Navamsa Chart which has a role to play in the stock market forecasting as will be seen in Chapter 3.

Navamsa Charts and How to Create Them. The word Navamsa in Sanskrit means $1/9^{th}$ part. As already stated, the Rasi chart forms the basic chart from which the Navamsa chart is derived. The sign in the Rasi chart comprising of 30^0 is further sub-divided into 9 parts, each part having an arc length of 30^0 20'. The first exercise is to divide the signs into 9 parts as shown below:

First Navamsa ---- 0^0 to 3^0 20'
Second Navamsa ---- 3^0 20' to 6^0 40'
Third Navamsa ---- 6^0 40' to 10^0 deg 0'
Fourth Navamsa ---- 10^0 0' to 13^0 20'
Fifth Navamsa ---- 13^0 20' to 16^0 40'
Sixth Navamsa ---- 16^0 40' to 20^0 0'
Seventh Navamsa ---- 20^0 0' to 23^0 20'
Eighth Navamsa ---- 23^0 20' to 26^0 40'
Ninth Navamsa ---- 26^0 40' to 30^0 0'

Thus, once we know the longitude of the planet concerned or the ascendant, we can place that planet or the ascendant in the correct Navamsa of the sign concerned. The rule to be followed for the preparation of Navamsa charts are:

A TYPICAL CHART AS USED IN SOUTH INDIA

PISCES ♓	ARIES ♈	TAURUS ♉	GEMINI ♊
AQUARIUS ♒	RASI CHART		CANCER ♋
CAPRICORN ♑			LEO ♌
SAGITTARIUS ♐	SCORPIO ♏	LIBRA ♎	VIRGO ♍

SIDEREAL LONGITUDES	
PLANET	DEGREES IN SIGN
ASCENDANT	
SUN	
MOON	
MARS	
MERCURY	
JUPITER	
VENUS	
SATURN	
RAHU	
KETU	
URANUS	
NEPTUNE	
PLUTO	

Chart # 1

a) For any planet posited in the signs of Aries, Leo and Sagittarius the Navamsa position is to be determined after counting the Navamsa from Aries.

b) For any planet posited in the signs of Taurus, Virgo and Capricorn the Navamsa position is to be determined by counting the Navamsa from Capricorn.

c) For any planet posited in the signs of Gemini, Libra and Aquarius the Navamsa position is to be determined by counting the Navamsa from Libra.

d) For any planet posited in the signs of Cancer, Scorpio and Pisces the Navamsa position is to be determined by counting the Navamsa from Cancer.

Thus each Sign will have nine Navamsas and taking all the 12 signs together we have the Zodiac divided into 108 Navamsas. Each Navamsa will also correspond to Nakshatra padas which are 108 in number.

Ashtaka Varga Charts. Ashtaka Varga chart is also derived from the basic Rasi chart. This chart has numerical values which help to evaluate easily the bullish and bearish trends in the stock markets. For this purpose we make out the Ashtaka Varga Chart of the New York Stock Exchange based on the Rasi chart of NYSE. The methodology of deriving the Ashtaka varga charts are explained in detail in the book "Vedic Astrology - Ashtaka Varga made simple for the Western Astrologer" by the same author. (Please refer to the Bibliography.) Many Vedic Astrology software programs can help in preparing the Ashtaka Varga Charts.

In Chapter 3, the method of evaluating the Stock Market based on the Ashtaka varga Chart of NYSE is discussed in detail.

Panchak Phenomenon. The Sanskrit word "Panchak" means five. The panchak phenomenon occurs whenever Moon transits the five consecutive Nakshatras namely, the padas 3 and 4 of

Dhanishta, and all the 4 padas of Satabisha, Poorva Bhadrapada, Uttara Bhadrapada and Revathi which are posited in Aquarius and Pisces. This phenomenon occurs every month on a 27 day cycle and lasts for five consecutive days. It is observed that whenever the panchak phenomenon is operative, the stock market has either a pronounced bullish or a bearish effect. The method of evaluation of the stock markets based on panchak phenomenon is discussed in detail, in Chapter 3.

Quadrants: Counting from the sign occupied by the ascendant, the 1st, 4th, 7th and the 10th houses are called the quadrants.

Trines. Counting from the sign in which the ascendant is placed, the 5th and the 9th signs therefrom are called trines.

Aspects. In Vedic Astrology, aspects are considered sign-wise. All planets aspect the planet(s) in the same sign as well as the 7th sign where they are posited regardless of the degree of longitudes of the planets concerned.

In addition to the 7th house aspect the following planets have additional full aspects.

Jupiter will aspect fully the 5th, 7th and 9th signs and the planet(s) posited therein from the sign it is posited.

Mars will aspect the 4th, 7th and 8th signs from where it is posited and the planet(s) posited in those signs.

Saturn will aspect the 3rd, 7th and 10th signs from where it is posited and the planet(s) posited in those signs.

Rahu and Ketu will aspect the 5th, 7th and 9th signs from where it is posited and the planet(s) posited in those signs.

Vedic Astrology Software: Many Vedic Astrology programs are currently available in the market. Some of the important ones are 'Parasara Light' and ‘Goravani Jyotish’.

Readers who are laymen can benefit a lot by using one of these programs as they can cast the horoscope for any date, time and place. Readers not conversant with Vedic Astrology and who have interest in Vedic Astrology can benefit by studying the correspondence course referenced in the Bibliography.

Use of Sidereal Ephemeris: The Betz Sidereal Ephemeris 1940 - 2040 is a good Ephemeris, which can be easily understood by a layman. After one gets conversant with the use of Ephemeris it will be easy to track planetary conjunctions and oppositions that will happen in the future and arrive at proper conclusions about the market trends both short term and long term well in advance.

B) Planetary Situations in Natal Charts, which are Conducive to Success in Stock Market Dealings.

Each one of us wants to provide for the future by building a nest egg. Generally, the investments are made in real estate, gold, bonds, bank deposits (CDs) or investments in stocks. As compared with other investments the investment in stock markets is a risky one. It is seen in practice that only a few people can succeed in making money on the stock market trading. The question that will naturally arise is who is best suited for the stock market dealings? Here, the Vedic Astrology seems to have the answ

The second house in any natal chart indicates the money and wealth that will be made by one's own efforts. The trinal houses namely the 5th and the 9th houses give information regarding money to be made through speculative deals like dealings in stock markets. The 11th house gives information about gains that are likely to be made. To succeed in stock market speculative deals one should have the Natal Chart in which the above mentioned wealth giving houses are rendered very strong due to placement of benefics. The best situation is the placement of the lord of the 5th house in the fifth house itself and placement of the lord of the 9th house in the ninth house itself. The other good situation is the Moon and Jupiter placed in a mutually trine position with each being placed in its own sign.

There are several combinations in the natal charts, which are conducive for a good cash flow through speculative deals culled from the classics. They are:

a) Moon, Jupiter, lords of the 2nd, 4th, 9th and the 11th houses are well placed in both Rasi and Navamsa charts.

b) Lords of the 2nd, 4th and the 9th houses are well placed and aspected by Moon.

c) Lords of the 2nd and the 9th houses are posited in the 11th house along with Moon and Jupiter.

d) Lord of the second house placed in the 11th house and lord of the eleventh house placed in the second house. This is called 'parivarthana yoga' involving the 2nd and the 11th houses.

e) Jupiter strongly placed in the ascendant and aspected by the lord of the 2nd, 5th and 9th houses.

f) Lord of the 2nd house exalted and placed in the 5th house along with the lord of the ascendant.

g) Both the lords of the 2nd house and the fifth house placed in the 11th house.

h) Mutual exchange of houses between the 2nd and 11th house lords, or the 5th and 11th lords, or the lords of the 2nd and 5th houses.

i) In the sarvashtaka varga chart the 11th house should have very large bindus and the 12th house should have the least number of bindus.

C) Classification of signs into Bullish and Bearish signs.

The 12 zodiacal signs can be broadly divided into bullish and bearish signs.

Bullish Signs: Aries, Taurus, Cancer, Leo, Libra, Scorpio, Sagittarius and Pisces are bullish signs. Whenever a benefic or a malefic planet(s) transits these signs, bullish trends are likely in the markets.

Bearish Signs: Gemini, Virgo, Capricorn and Aquarius are considered as bearish signs. Whenever a benefic or a malefic planet(s) transits these signs, bearish trends are likely in the markets.

Chapter Two

Do Planetary Transits Impact the Market Trends?

In the remote past, as early as 505A.D, the great Varaha Mihira who was an Astronomer-cum Astrologer had enunciated in his treatise "Brihat Samhita", that price fluctuations in the market are related to planetary movements along the Zodiac.

The great classics of Vedic Astrology have stated that the slow moving planets like Jupiter, Saturn, Rahu and Ketu as they transit each sign do impact the market trends one way or the other. These transits recur at regular intervals of time known as a 'planetary cycle'. For example, Jupiter will transit the same sign at a regular interval of 12 yrs, Saturn will transit the same sign at a regular interval of 30 yrs and Rahu and Ketu transit the same sign at a regular interval of 18 yrs. Thus, there is a broad pattern of planetary cycles arising out of the movement of slow moving planets which do have an impact on the market trends.

In the last three centuries, many western thinkers, economists, and astronomers had applied their minds to the phenomenon of market trends. The economists had related the price to function of demand versus supply but were unable to explain why the demand and supply position varied from time to time.
Sir William Herschel, the astronomer who discovered the planet Uranus had stated in the year 1801, that there appeared to be some relationship between sunspots and the price of wheat. Later in the year 1875, Samuel Benner evolved his theory about price cycles and advocated a 11 year cycle affected all business activity. Later, Prof. H.L. Moore of Columbia University had developed a "Moore's 8 year Venus cycle which followed closely the inferior conjunction of Venus. In 1938, Louise McWhirter had advanced a theory of business cycle of 19 years studying the Moon's nodes

from the above it will be seen that there exists a cycle which affects business activity periodically.

In the classics of Vedic Astrology, some information is available about the effects of slow moving planets as they sojourn transiting sign to sign in their orbital movement. They are discussed below. Readers are cautioned that the effects described in the classics are concerning certain commodities like food grains etc. Since general price fluctuations in the markets regarding other commodities also affect the stock markets the author is of the opinion that the effects described below also have a bearing on the stock market trends.

Effects of Jupiter's Transit through the 12 zodial signs.

Aries: Jupiter's transit through Aries generally causes bearish trends when Jupiter is in direct motion but when Jupiter gets retrograde bullish trends are caused.

Taurus: Jupiter's transit through Taurus generally causes good bullish trends both during direct as well as in retrograde motion.
Gemini: Jupiter's transit through Gemini generally causes bearish trends but when Jupiter becomes retrograde bullish trends are activated.

Cancer: Jupiter's transit through Cancer generally causes bullish trend when Jupiter is in retrograde motion and causes bearish trends when Jupiter in direct motion.

Leo: Jupiter's transit in Leo generally causes bullish trends during its direct motion, whereas bearish trends are caused during its retrograde motion.

Virgo: Jupiter 's transit through Virgo generally causes bullish trends while in retrograde motion and bearish trends while in direct motion.

Libra: Jupiter's transit through Libra generally causes bullish trends while in retrograde motion and bearish trends while in direct motion.

Scorpio: Jupiter's transit in Scorpio generally causes bullish trends during its retrograde motion and bearish trends while in direct motion.

Sagittarius: Jupiter's transit through Sagittarius generally causes bullish trends while in direct motion and bearish trends while in retrogression.

Capricorn: Jupiter's transit in Capricorn generally causes bullish condition during both direct as well as in retrograde motion.

Aquarius: Jupiter's transit through Aquarius generally causes bullish trends while in direct motion and bearish trends while in retrogression.

Pisces: Jupiter's transit in Pisces generally causes bullish trends both in direct as well as retrograde motion.

Effects of Saturn's Transit through the 12 Zodiacal Signs:

Aries:Saturn's transit through Aries generally causes bullish trends both in direct as well as in retrograde motion.

Taurus: Saturn's transit through Taurus generally causes bullish trends while in retrogression but when Saturn becomes direct, the bullish trend gets very much subdued.

Gemini: Saturn's transit through Gemini generally causes volatile situation - some times bullish trends and some times bearish trends while in direct as well as retrograde motion.

Cancer: Saturn's transit through Cancer causes volatile conditions which means sometimes bullish and sometimes bearish trends while in retrogression and bearish trends while in direct motion.

Leo: Saturn's transit through Leo causes bullish trends during its retrogression and bearish trends when it is direct.

Virgo: Saturn's transit through Virgo causes bullish trends during its retrogression and volatile trends when it is direct.

Libra: Saturn's transit through Libra causes bullish trends during either direct or retrograde motion.
Scorpio: Saturn's transit through Scorpio causes bullish trends when Saturn is retrograde and causes bearish trends when Saturn becomes direct.

Sagittarius: Saturn's transit through Sagittarius causes bullish trends when it is retrograde and bearish when it becomes direct.

Capricorn: Saturn's transit in Capricorn causes volatile conditions when direct and causes bearish trends when it becomes retrograde.

Aquarius: Saturn's transit through Aquarius causes volatile conditions during Saturn's direct as well retrograde motions.

Pisces: Saturn's transit through Pisces causes volatile conditions when Saturn is direct and bullish conditions when Saturn becomes retrograde.

Effects of Rahu and Ketu's Transit through the 12 Zodiacal Signs:

Rahu and Ketu are posited at 180^0 apart and they always move anticlockwise, together. If Rahu transits one sign then Ketu will be in the 7th sign from it. The effect of the transits of Rahu and Ketu through the 12 zodiacal signs are given below.

Aries: Rahu's transit through Aries causes bullish trends.

Taurus: Rahu's transit through Taurus causes bullish trends.

Gemini: Rahu's transit through Gemini causes bearish conditions.

Cancer: Rahu's transit through Cancer causes bullish trends.

Leo: Rahu's transit through Leo causes bullish trends.

Virgo: Rahu's transit through Virgo causes bullish trends.

Libra: Rahu's transit through Libra causes bullish trends.

Scorpio: Rahu's transit through Scorpio causes volatile conditions.

Sagittarius: Rahu's transit through Sagittarius causes volatile conditions.

Capricorn: Rahu's transit in Capricorn causes bearish conditions.

Aquarius: Rahu's transit through Aquarius causes bullish conditions.

Pisces: Rahu's transit through Pisces causes bearish conditions.

Hindu years and their relevance to market trends:

There are 60 names of Hindu years which repeat on a 60 yr cycle. Each year has a distinct name and each year is believed to cause certain distinct effect on the economy as it repeats every 60 yrs. In some parts of India where Lunar system is followed, the New Year commences on the next day after the Lunation in Pisces. Every Hindu Almanac, called the "Panchang", will give this day much importance and festivals are celebrated on this day. The Astrological chart prepared for the Lunation in Pisces for the country concerned gives information regarding the shape of things to come in the new year. This is discussed under the heading "Lunation Charts", in Chapter 3.

In some parts of India, a solar system is followed. Here, the day when Sun enters the first point of Aries is considered as the commencement of the New Year. The Solar ingress charts made out for the entry of Sun in the sign of Aries for the country concerned gives information regarding the shape of things to come in the New Year. These are discussed under the heading "Solar ingress charts" in Chapter 3. It is the custom with most of the Indian house holds to read the "Panchang" on the New Year day and to learn about the situation that are likely in the New Year as stated in the Panchang which are in turn based on the analysis of the Lunation and Solar ingress charts as mentioned above.

The 60 Hindu Years and the Situations that are likely in these years as stated in the Vedic Astrological Classics.

For the benefit of the readers the corresponding year as per Gregarian Calendar is given in parenthesis. As stated above, the Hindu New year (lunar based) will commence on the next day of Lunation in the sign of Pisces which will be in the month of March/April of the Gregorian year concerned and The Hindu Year (solar based) will commence in the month of April of the Gregorian year concerned.

1) Prabhava (1927, 1987, 2047 etc): This likely to be a bad year. People are likely to experience hardships like drought, storms, hurricanes and other natural calamities.

2) Vibhava (1928, 1968, 2048 etc.)
3) Sukla (1929, 1989, 2049 etc.)
4) Promoduta (1930, 1090, 2050 etc.)
5) Prajotpatti (1931, 1991, 2051 etc.)

These four consecutive years are likely to be good years. People will experience peace and prosperity.

6) Angirasa (1932, 1992, 2052 etc.)
7) Srimukha (1933, 1993, 2053 etc.)
8) Bhava (1934, 1994, 2054 etc.)

These three consecutive years are likely to be good years. People will experience peace and prosperity.

9) Yuva (1935, 1995, 2055 etc.)
10) Dhatu (1936, 1996, 2056 etc.)

These two years likely to be two bad years in a row. People will be prone to fear of wars, fear of epidemics etc.

11) Iswara (1937, 1997, 2057 etc.)
12) Bahudanya (1938, 1998, 2058 etc.)

These two years will be very good years. People will experience peace and prosperity.

13) **Pramadi (1939, 1999, 2059)** This year is likely to be a bad year. People are prone to experience several hardships in their lives.

14) Vikrama (1940, 2000, 2060 etc.)
15) Vishu (1941, 2001, 2061 etc.)

These years are likely to be problematic years. People will be gripped with fear due to several uncertain developments.

16) Chitrabhanu (1942, 2002, 2062 etc.) This year is likely to be a good year. People will experience many happy developments.

17) Swabhanu (1943, 2003, 2063 etc.) This is likely to be a bad year. People will be prone to fear of epidemics and also large number of deaths.

18) Tarana (1944, 2004, 2064 etc.)
19) Parthibha (1945,2005, 2065 etc.)

These two consecutive years are likely to be very good years. People will experience peace and prosperity.

20) Vyaya (1946, 2006, 2066 etc.) This is likely to be a good year. People will experience more prosperity.

21) Sarvajit (1947, 2007, 2067 etc.)

This is likely to be a bad year. People will be prone to many setbacks and sufferings.

22) Sarvadhari (1948, 2008, 2068 etc.) This is likely be a good year. People will experience much relief and many happy developments.

23) Virodhi (1949, 2009, 2069 etc)
24) Vikruti (1950, 2010, 2070 etc.)
25) Khara (1951, 2011, 2071 etc.)

These three years are likely to be three bad years in a row. People will be prone to many problems concerning their livelihood.

26) Nandana (1952, 2012, 2072 etc.)
27) Vijaya (1953, 2013, 2073 etc.)
28) Jaya (1954, 2014, 2074 etc.)

These three consecutive years are likely to be three good years in a row. People will feel a lot of relief and enjoy peace and prosperity.

29) Manmatha (1955, 2015, 2075 etc.)

This year is likely to be a good as well as a bad year. People are likely to experience uncertainties in everything while enjoying their prosperity.

30) Durmukhi (1956, 2016, 2076 etc.)
31) Hevilambhi (1957, 2017, 2077 etc.)
32) Vilambhi (1958, 2018, 2078 etc.)
33) Vikari (1959, 2019, 2079 etc.)
34) Sarvari (1960, 2020, 2080 etc.)

These are likely to be 5 consecutive bad years in a row.

People will be prone to natural calamities and several hardships.

35) Plava (1961, 2021, 2081 etc.)
36) Subhakrit (1962, 2022, 2082 etc.)
37) Shobakrit (1963, 2023, 2083 etc.)

These three consecutive years are likely to be good years.People will experience relief from earlier hardships and are likely to experience peace and prosperity.

38) Krodhi (1964, 2024, 2084 etc.)
39) Viswavasu (1965, 2025, 2085 etc.)
40) Prabhava (1966, 2026, 2086 etc.)
41) Plavanga (1967, 2027, 2087 etc.)

These four consecutive years are likely to be bad years. People will be prone to epidemics, natural calamities and several hardships.

42) Keelaka (1968, 2028, 2088 etc.)
43) Soumya (1969, 2029, 2089 etc.)

These two years are likely to be good years. People will get lots of relief from earlier problems and are likely to experience many happy developments.

44) Sadharana (1970, 2030, 2090 etc.) This is likely to be a bad year. People will be prone to many problems.

45) Virodhikrit (1971, 2031, 2091 etc.) This is likely to be a good year. People will experience relief from problems and also experience prosperity.

46) Paridhabhi (1972, 2032, 2092 etc.) This is likely to be a bad year. People will be prone to natural calamities. A national mourning is also likely.

47) Pramadhicha (1973, 2033, 2093 etc.) This is likely to be a bad year. People will be prone to many fears including fear of war.

48) Ananda (1974, 2034, 2094 etc.) This is likely to be a good year. People will enjoy peace and prosperity.

49) Rakshasa (1975, 2035, 2095 etc.)
50) Nala (1976, 2036, 2096 etc.)
51) Pingala (1977, 2037, 2097 etc.)
52) Kalayukthi (1978, 2038, 2098 etc.)

These 4 consecutive years are likely to be bad years. People will be prone to natural calamities, epidemics and also fear of war.

53) Siddharthi (1979, 2039, 2099 etc.) This is likely to be a good year. People will be free from problems and will experience peace and prosperity.

54) Rowdhri (1980,2040, 3000 etc.)
55) Dhurmathi (1981,2041,3001 etc.)

These is likely to be two bad years in a row. People will be prone to natural calamities and suffering.

56) Dhundhubhi (1982, 2042, 3002 etc.) This is likely to be a good year. People will feel relief from their problems and experience prosperity.

57) Rudhrothghari (1983, 2043, 3003 etc.)
58) Raktashi Akshaya (1984, 2044, 3004 etc.)
59) Krodhana (1985, 2045, 3005 etc.)
60) Akshaya (1986, 2046, 3006 etc.)

These are likely to be 3 bad years in a row. People will be prone to natural calamities, war and epidemics.

How to Evaluate Long-Term Trends in the Stock Markets: Readers are aware that all planets as they go around the orbit conjunct with other planets from time to time. These conjunctions do have an impact on the market. It is also observed that the markets trends are affected by these conjunctions.

Slow moving planets like Jupiter, Saturn, Rahu and Ketu conjunct periodically and this conjunction helps to infer long-term trends in the markets.

The outer planets like Uranus, Neptune and Pluto also periodically conjunct with slow moving planets and these also help to infer the long-term trends ahead of the conjunction.
Conjunctions between slow moving planets affect the short term trends in the stock market. Some of these conjunctions are

discussed below.

a) Saturn-Jupiter Conjunction and Opposition and its Long Term Effects: Slow moving planets like Saturn and Jupiter are helpful in delineating long-term trends. Readers are aware that Saturn moves slowly and completes its orbit in a period of 30 years. Similarly, Jupiter moves on a 12 year cycle. It is also seen that Jupiter and Saturn conjunct every 20 years and oppose each other every 20 years. Thus, the Saturn-Jupiter conjunction or opposition takes place every 10 years. This phenomenon, whenever it takes place makes the economy of all countries prone to problems in the year of its happening. In particular, the stock markets in all countries become volatile during the period of operation of conjunction of Jupiter and Saturn in any sign (in Vedic Astrology if two planets are posited in one sign a conjunction occurs between them, regardless of their longitudes in that sign).

In the past, Saturn-Jupiter conjunctions on the same longitude occurred on 5/28/2000, 12/25/1980, 2/18/1961, 8/4/1940, 9/12/1921 and 11/30/1901.

Let us examine the situations around the above dates. On 5/28/2000, a Sunday, stock markets were closed. The DJIA numbers in this period were:

3/24/2000 -------- 11, 112.73
4/26/2000 -------- 10, 945.50
5/26/2000 -------- 10, 299.26
6/26/2000 -------- 10, 543.00

This indicates a high degree of volatility ain the markets round the exact conjunction date.

On 12/25/1980, Christmas day, markets were closed. DJIA numbers in this period were:

11/21/1980 -------- 989.93
12/23/1980 -------- 958.28
1/26/1981 -------- 938.91

Stock markets were closed on 2/18/1961, a Saturday. DJIA numbers in this period were:

1/18/1961 -------- 634.10
2/17/1961 -------- 651.67
3/17/1961 -------- 676.48

On 8/4/1940, a Sunday, stock markets were closed. DJIA in this period were:

7/6/1940 -------- 121.59
8/5/1940 -------- 126.44
9/4/1940 -------- 132.16

On 9/12/1921, stock markets were open. DJIA numbers in this period were:

8/12/1921 -------- 66.88
9/12/1921 -------- 70.68
10/10/1921 -------- 70.95

On 11/30/1901 stock markets were open. DJIA numbers in this period were:

10/30/1901 -------- 64.86
11.30/1901 -------- 65.01
12/30/1901 -------- 63.33

The above cases indicate that the markets were volatile around the period of Jupiter-Saturn conjunction on the same longitude.

Jupiter-Saturn opposition occurs every 20 years. In the past such an opposition occurred on the same longitude on 7/13/1990, 12/29/1969, 10/15/1951, 7/26/1930 and 11/18/1910.

Let us examine the situation of the markets around these periods. On 7/13/1990, stock markets were open. DJIA numbers in this period were:

6/13/1990 -------- 2, 929.70
7/13/1990 -------- 2, 980.20
8/13/1990 -------- 2, 746.78

On 10/29/1969, stock markets were open. DJIA numbers in this period were:

9/29/1969 -------- 818.04
10/29/1969 -------- 848.34
11/28/1969 -------- 812.30

On 10/15/1951 stock markets were open. DJIA numbers in this period were:

9/14/1951 -------- 276.06
10/15/1951 -------- 275.74
11/15/1951 -------- 260.91

On 7/26/1930 stock markets were open. DJIA numbers in this period were:

6/26/1930 -------- 220.58
7/26/1930 -------- 240.31
8/27/1930 -------- 237.93

On 11/18/1910, stock markets were open. DJIA numbers in this period were:

10/18/1910 --------- 86.02
11/18/1910 --------- 85.12
12/19/1910 --------- 82.16

B) Some Important Conjunctions involving Slow Moving and Outer Planets.

The ancient Rishis who enunciated the principles of Vedic Astrology more than 5000 years ago had based their observations on the nine planets namely, Sun, Moon, Mars, Mercury, Jupiter, Saturn, Rahu and Ketu. These principles had stood the test of time and are found to be valid even to day. However, with the discovery of the outer planets like Uranus, Neptune and Pluto it is observed in practice that these planets also have effects on the stock markets, particularly when they conjunct traditional nine planets. Some of these conjunctions which take place periodically are listed below. These conjunctions have an effect on the stock market. It has been observed that the market trends change soon after each conjunction. The conjunctions involving Jupiter generally brings about bullish trends in the stock markets and the conjunctions involving Saturn generally brings about bearish trends in the stock market.

It is also noticed that these conjunctions have an impact on the shares of those companies that fall under the significations of these planets and under the significations of the zodiacal signs in which these conjunctions take place. Using an Ephemeris It is possible to work out such planetary conjunctions in advance and arrive at proper conclusions regarding the behavior of stock markets down the road.

Some important conjunctions of slow moving planets are given below along with the frequency in which these conjunctions occur.

Jupiter-Uranus Conjunction: Takes place once in 13.81 yrs and is conducive to bullish trends in the market.

Jupiter-Neptune Conjunction: This takes place once in 12.78 yrs and is conducive to bullish trends in the market.

Jupiter-Pluto Conjunction: This takes place once in 12.45 yrs and is conducive to bullish trend in the market.

Jupiter-Rahu Conjunction: This takes place once in about 7 yrs and is conducive to bullish trends in the market.

Jupiter-Ketu Conjunction: This takes place once in about 7 yrs and is conducive to bearish trends in the market.

Saturn-Uranus Conjunction: This takes place once in 45.36 yrs and is conducive to bullish trends in the market.

Saturn-Neptune Conjunction: This takes place once in about 35.86 yrs and is conducive to bullish trends in the market.

Saturn-Pluto Conjunction: This takes place once in 33.43 yrs and is conducive to bearish trends in the market.

Saturn-Rahu conjunction: This takes place once in about 12 yrs and is conducive to bullish trends in the market.

Saturn - Ketu conjunction: This takes place once in 12 yrs and is conducive to bearish trends in the market.

Other Important Conjunctions of Planets, which affect the Stock Markets.

There are other conjunctions involving fast moving planets which conjunct at shorter intervals. These are listed below with their effects on the markets.

Mars-Jupiter Conjunction: This conjunction takes place every 27th month. This conjunction has bullish effects on the market. The last such conjunction occurred on 4/6/2000 and the next such conjunction is due on 7/4/2002. The DJIA numbers close to the conjunction date of 4/6/2000 are:

3/30/2000 ------- 10, 980.25
4/6/2000 ------- 11, 114.27
4/7/2000 ------- 11, 111.48

Saturn-Mars Conjunction: This occurs once in about every 2 years. This conjunction has a tendency to make the stock market volatile and very often the stock market gets into a bearish trend close to the conjunction on the same degree of longitude.

During the period of 3/15/2000 to 4/26/2000 both Mars and Saturn were conjunct in Aries. And they were conjunct withe same degree of longitude on 4/16/2000, being a Sunday, the stock markets were closed.

The DJIA numbers on the days close to this conjunction were:

4/10/2000 -------- 11, 186.56
4/17/2000 -------- 10, 582.51
4/19/2000 -------- 10, 674.96

Venus-Jupiter Conjunction: This occurs roughly every 223 days and this generally has a bullish effect on the markets. Recently both Venus and Jupiter were conjunct on the same degree of longitude on 5/18/2000. The DJIA numbers close to this conjunction date were:

5/12/2000 -------- 10, 609.37
5/18/2000 -------- 10, 777.28

The above are some of the planetary conjunctions, which have an effect on the stock market. Apart from these conjunctions, there are also conjunctions with the outer planets which take place from time to time. However, of these conjunctions, those involving Mercury or Venus have an impact on the markets. They are: Venus-Uranus, Venus-Neptune,Venus-Pluto, Mercury-Uranus, Mercury-Neptune and Mercury-Pluto.

Multiple Planetary Conjunctions: Sometimes many planets congregate in one sign and this causes sign conjunction which means that all the planets are in one sign but not necessarily on the same degree of

longitude. Such multiple planetary conjunctions in any sign causes imbalance on the market forces.

On 2/4/1962, a Sunday, a conjunction of eight planets took place in the sign of Capricorn (sidereal). The DJIA numbers close to this conjunction date were:

1/4/1962 ------- 722.50
2/5/1962 ------- 706.10
3/2/1962 ------- 711

Recently on 5/3/2000 we had six planets in the sign Aries (Chart # 2). Readers are aware of the market fluctuations following this conjunction. The DJIA numbers around this date are as under:

5/1/2000 ------- 10, 811.78
5/3/2000 ------- 10, 480.13
6/3/2000 ------- 10, 577.80

The above figures indicate the market fluctuations at that point of time following the conjunction.

Down the road, a 7 planet conjunction is due to take place in Taurus (sidereal) on 5/14/2002. This conjunction is likely to make the market forces highly volatile.

SIX PLANET COMBINATION

5/2/2000 14:32 (EDT) WASHINGTON D.C.

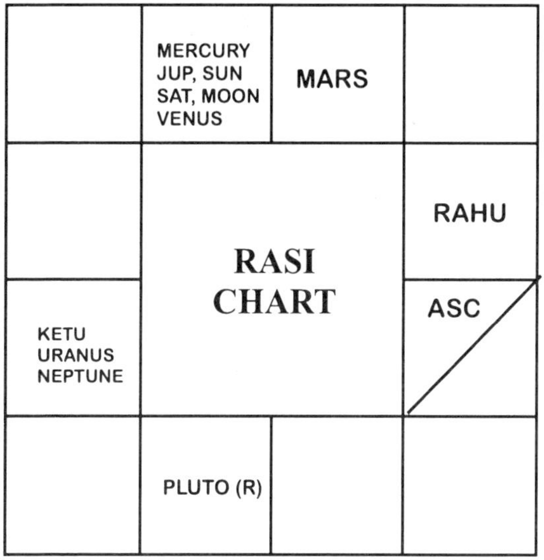

SIDEREAL LONGITUDES	
PLANET	DEGREES IN SIGN
ASCENDANT	♌ 13° - 33'
SUN	♈ 18° - 47'
MOON	♈ 0° - 0'
MARS	♉ 5° - 25'
MERCURY	♈ 11° - 25'
JUPITER	♈ 22° - 44'
VENUS	♈ 9° - 10'
SATURN	♈ 25° - 32'
RAHU	♋ 3° - 54'
KETU	♑ 3° - 54'
URANUS	♑ 26° - 45'
NEPTUNE	♑ 12° - 42'
PLUTO (R)	♏ 18° - 26'

Chart # 2

Chapter Three

How to Evaluate Short-Term Projections in Stock Market.

Short term projections of the stock market is rather difficult as several factors have to be taken into account and it is difficult to comprehend the sum total effects of all these factors. By repeated applications and practice one can do a reasonably accurate forecast of short-term trends in the market.

Eclipses and Their Effects on the Stock Market.

It is generally seen that eclipses, both solar and lunar, have an impact on the markets whenever they occur. Solar eclipses always take place on lunation days or new moon days and lunar eclipses always take place on full moon days. The effects of these eclipses are more valid in the countries in which the eclipses are visible and also in the countries ruled by the signs in which the eclipses take place. It is also believed that the effects of solar eclipses will be operative over a period in years equal to the duration of the eclipse in hours. In the case of lunar eclipses it is believed the effects will be operative for period in months equal to the duration of the eclipse in hours. The following are some of the general effects that are likely when eclipses fall on movable signs, fixed signs and common signs.

Eclipses falling on Cardinal signs namely, Aries, Cancer, Libra and Capricorn: Crop failure, trade problems and political problems likely.

Eclipses falling on Fixed signs namely, Taurus, Leo, Scorpio and Aquarius: Accidents, labor problems, epidemics and death of a prominent leader or person likely.

Eclipses falling on Common signs namely, Gemini, Virgo, Sagittarius and Pisces: Increase in crime, conflicts and unrest concerning religion are likely. The following are the general effects when eclipses fall on Fiery, Earth, Airy and Watery signs.

Eclipses falling on Fiery signs namely, Aries, Leo and Sagittarius: Death of top a political leader, drought, higher taxes and danger of wars are likely.

Eclipses falling on Earthy Signs namely, Taurus, Virgo, and Capricorn: Crop failure, down turn in economy etc. are likely.
Eclipses falling on Airy Signs namely, Gemini, Libra and Aquarius.

Thunder storms, hurricanes, internal unrest in nations likely.

Eclipses falling on Watery signs namely, Cancer, Scorpio and Pisces: Heavy rainfall, havoc by floods, large-scale deaths due to drowning, large-scale epidemics are likely.

How to make an Eclipse chart: As mentioned earlier a solar eclipse takes place on a lunation day. Therefore, the solar eclipse chart has to be made for the exact time Sun and Moon will be conjunct on the same degree with reference to the place in question. Normally we consider the capital of the country to make the eclipse chart for that country. Similarly, the capital of a state should be considered for making an eclipse chart for a particular state.

As stated earlier, lunar eclipse always takes place on a full moon day The chart for lunar eclipse has to be made for the exact time when Sun and Moon will be in opposition on the same degree of longitude at the place concerned.

How to Evaluate an Eclipse Chart: The signification of the various houses will be similar to the ones which apply to natal charts of individuals.

However, mundane charts indicate the state of a nation or the country including the economy. Broadly, the significations of the various houses are given below. These significations apply to the country as a whole or the region as a whole. While applying these principles to the stock markets we have to infer the possible effects of each house on the economy as whole and arrive at our conclusions. These broad indications also apply to other mundane charts like lunation and solar ingress charts.

First House: Signifies the state of the nation. Broadly speaking, the presence of benefics indicates political stability and a healthy economy while the presence of malefics indicates political instability and a sick economy.

Second House: This is an important house having a direct bearing on the stock markets. Broadly speaking, the presence of benefics indicates a good consumer confidence and bullish conditions in the stock market while the presence of malefics indicates a lack of consumer confidence and bearish conditions in the market.

Third House: Signifies the means of communications like railroads, airways waterways and also the electronic media, print media radio and television. Presence of benefics denotes better communication facilities, which in turn will have a favorable effect on the economy and the stock market.The presence of malefics indicates some Deadlocks and communication gaps, scandals which make headlines and such matters which may have an adverse effect on the economy and the stock market.

Fourth House: Signifies the real estate, crop prospects natural disasters like earthquakes, storms and very adverse weather conditions, behavior of the opposition who often make a political capital out of adverse condition etc. Presence of benefics denotes a favorable environment in regard to the above which have a favorable effect on the economy and the market. Presence of malefics denotes adverse conditions in regard to the economy and the markets.

Fifth House: Signifies all forms of entertainment like cinema, radio and television, lotteries, casinos and matters concerning the incumbent of the highest political office. Presence of benefic indicates a favorable situation in regard to the above, which in turn will help to boost the consumer confidence, economy and the market. Presence of malefics denotes adverse conditions in regard to the above including danger to the person holding the highest political office and such factors which will adversely affect consumer confidence, state of economy and the markets.

Sixth House: Signifies war like conditions, public debt, labor unrest, unrest of people in general, unemployment situation, unemployment claims, general hygiene, sanitary

conditions and proneness of human and cattle population to epidemics, large scale death etc.

Presence of benefics indicates favorable conditions in regard to the above, which has a positive effect on the economy and the markets. Presence of malefics indicates adverse conditions in regard to the above, which have negative impact on the economy and the markets.

Seventh House: Signifies diplomacy, relationship with foreign countries, disputes with other countries and foreign trade, trade war and also war with other countries.

Presence of benefics denotes favorable developments in the above areas, which in turn will have a positive effect on the economy and the markets. Presence of malefics denotes problems in the areas indicated above which in turn will have a negative effect on the economy and the markets.

Eighth House: Signifies stability of government, danger to life of the incumbent of the highest political office, foreign debt, natural disasters, famines, epidemics and large-scale deaths of people through such calamities. Presence of benefic denotes favorable developments in the above areas, which in turn will have positive impact on the economy and the markets. Presence of malefic denotes adverse developments in the above areas, which in turn will have a negative impact on the economy and the markets.

Ninth House: Signifies exports and imports, tourism, media including print media, television, and radio, religious faith, religious bodies, and public relations of the Government. Presence of benefics denotes favorable developments in the above areas which in turn have positive impact on the economy and the markets. Presence of malefic denotes adverse developments in the above areas, with negative impact on the economy and the markets.

Tenth House: Signifies the incumbent of the top political office, the ruling party, prestige of the nation and the international image of the nation. Presence of benefic denotes favorable developments in the above areas, which in turn will have a favorable impact on the economy and the markets. Presence of malefic denotes adverse development in the above areas, which in turn will have a negative impact on the economy and the markets.

Eleventh house: Financial gains from international trade, balance of trade, diplomacy, ambassadors, relationship with foreign countries, stated goals of the government, lotteries and casinos. Placement of benefic denotes favorable developments in the above areas that in turn have a positive effect on the economy and the markets. Placement of malefics denotes adverse developments in the above areas, which in turn will have negative impact on the economy and the markets.

Twelfth house: Foreign spies, underground movements, terrorist's attacks on government, labor unrest, strikes by organized labor and scams of various nature. Presence of benefics indicates favorable developments in the above areas, which in turn will have a positive impact on the economy and the markets. Presence of malefic denotes adverse developments in the above areas, which in turn will have a negative impact on the economy and the markets.

Analysis of Some Typical Eclipse Charts.

a) Total Solar Eclipse on 8/11/1999 at 7:08 AM(EDT) at Washington DC.

Please see Chart# 3. It will be seen from this chart that the 9th house is rendered strong. Jupiter aspects the 2nd house. Saturn-Jupiter conjunction in the 9th house, aspected by yogakaraka Mars denotes a bullish trend ahead. The lunation is placed in the 12th house with Rahu and Mercury both being malefics. Further, the 12th house is aspected by Ketu, Uranus and Neptune. Pluto is adversely placed. Uranus, Neptune and Pluto are all in retrogression. This situation denotes volatile conditions in the market. DJIA numbers in the month before and after the Eclipse date are:

6/30/99 -------- 10, 970.80
8/11/99 -------- 10, 787.80
8/23/99 -------- 11, 299.76
9/23/99 -------- 10, 318.59

b) Lunar Eclipse on August 7, 1998 at 22:10 (EDT) at Washington DC.

Please see Chart # 4. The second house is afflicted due to Saturn being posited therein. Further, Venus lord of the 8th house is conjunct with the lord of the 9th house. Mars is in the 4th house. These were all negative indications. But the 11th house is rendered strong due to the placement of the lord of the 5th house there along with Uranus and Neptune. Pluto is also favorably placed. These are positive indications. All these indicate volatile conditions in the market. The DJIA numbers close to this eclipse date are:

8/5/1998 -------- 8, 546.77
8/6/1998 -------- 8, 577.67
8/7/1998 -------- 8, 598.01
8/8/1998 -------- Saturday-holiday
8/10/1998 -------- 8, 574.84
8/13/1998 -------- 8, 459.49

Solar Ingress Charts for Sun's entry into the 12 Zodiacal signs.

The chart prepared for the exact time of entry of Sun into any zodiacal sign is called Solar ingress. Each year the Sun generally enters the various zodiacal signs around the dates as given below.

TOTAL SOLAR ECLIPSE ON
8/11/1999 7:08 (EDT) WASHINGTON D.C.

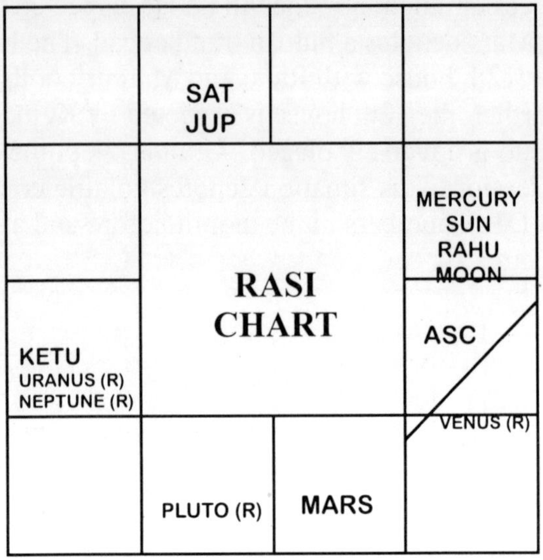

SIDEREAL LONGITUDES	
PLANET	DEGREES IN SIGN
ASCENDANT	♌ 3° - 35'
SUN	♋ 24° - 30'
MOON	♋ 24° - 30'
MARS	♎ 23° - 00'
MERCURY	♋ 6° - 18'
JUPITER	♈ 10° - 50'
VENUS (R)	♌ 8° - 18'
SATURN	♈ 23° - 01'
RAHU	♋ 19° - 06'
KETU	♑ 19° - 06'
URANUS (R)	♑ 20° - 49'
NEPTUNE (R)	♑ 8° - 42'
PLUTO (R)	♏ 13° - 54'

Chart # 3

LUNAR ECLIPSE

8/7/1998 22:10 (EDT) WASHINGTON D.C.

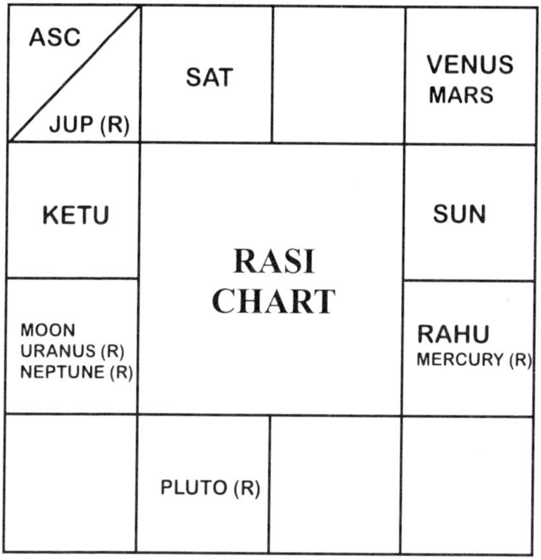

SIDEREAL LONGITUDES	
PLANET	**DEGREES IN SIGN**
ASCENDANT	♓ 9° - 16’
SUN	♋ 21° - 31’
MOON	♑ 21° - 31’
MARS	♊ 27° - 54’
MERCURY (R)	♌ 1° - 44’
JUPITER (R)	♓ 3° - 30’
VENUS	♊ 29° - 42’
SATURN	♈ 9° - 44’
RAHU	♌ 7° - 37’
KETU	♒ 7° - 37’
URANUS (R)	♑ 16° - 44’
NEPTUNE (R)	♑ 6° - 32’
PLUTO (R)	♏ 11° - 28’

Chart # 4

Aries on or near April 13 of that year.
Taurus on or near May 14 of that year.
Gemini on or near June 14 of that year.
Cancer on or near July 16 of that year.
Leo on or near August 16 of that year.
Virgo on or near September 16 of that year.
Libra on or near October 16 of that year.
Scorpio on or near November 15 of that year.
Sagittarius on or near December 15 of that year.
Capricorn on or near January 13 of that year.
Aquarius on or near February 12 of that year.
Pisces on or near March 14 of that year.

Sidereal ephemeris indicates the date on which Sun changes signs. These are the dates of solar ingress. The exact time of Sun's entry into any sign can be arrived at by further calculation. A simpler way is to use an astrology software to create a chart for the day of solar ingress with an assumed time. This chart should be edited further by altering the time in such a manner as to make the longitude of the Sun as $0^0$and 0' in that particular sign. The resultant chart is the solar ingress chart for Sun's entry into that particular sign.

Solar ingress charts for any sign should be made for the capital of a country for the time when Sun just enters the sign concerned. In this book we have prepared the solar ingress charts for Washington, D.C.

Evaluation of Solar Ingress Charts: These charts are to be evaluated based on the same principles given above for the evaluation of an eclipse chart. These solar ingress charts generally give information about the likely conditions for the next month following the day of solar ingress. Thus, these charts help in forecasting the short term market trends.

Analysis of the solar ingress charts for four movable signs namely, Aries, Cancer, Libra and Capricorn for the year 1999 is given below. Currently, various corporations report their earnings every quarter and these earnings reports play a major part in the behavior of the stock markets. The solar ingress chart for the Sun's entry into

Aries gives information regarding the quarter commencing in April and lasting until June. Similarly, the solar ingress chart for the Sun's entry into Cancer gives information regarding the quarter commencing in July and lasting until September. Solar ingress chart for Sun's entry into Libra gives information regarding the quarter commencing in October and lasting until December and the solar ingress chart for Sun's entry into Capricorn gives information for the quarter commencing in January and lasting until March. Some typical solar ingress charts are discussed below:

Solar ingress chart for Sun's entry into Aries on 4/14/1999 at 02:00 AM (EDT), Washington DC: Please see Chart# 5. The 4th house in this chart is rendered strong due to the placement of Jupiter in his own house there, along with Moon and Mercury. Lord of the 9th house (Sun) is well placed in the 5th house along with the lord of the 2nd house (Saturn). Mars, lord of the 5th house is well placed in the 11th house. These are all plus ponts. Rahu, Ketu, Uranus, Neptune and Pluto are all adversely placed. Venus is in trine with Ketu. These are all minus points. These indicate volatile conditions ahead in the market with a predominant upward trend. DJIA numbers close to the date of solar ingress are:

4/14/1999 -------- 10, 411.68
4/22/1999 -------- 10, 727.18
5/14/1999 -------- 10, 913.32
6/14/1999 -------- 10, 563.33

b) Solar ingress chart for Sun's entry into Cancer on 7/16/1999 at 16:00 (EDT), Washington DC: Please see Chart # 6. The lord of the 10th house Moon is favorably placed in the 11th house. Jupiter Saturn conjunction in the 9th house is also favorable. These are positive indications. However, the lord of the 11th house Sun is afflicted . Rahu and Kethu are also adversely placed. Furthermore, both Neptune and Uranus are retrograde and are also adversely placed. Venus who is also the lord of the 8th house is placed in the 11th house. All of the above suggest that the market is likely to become volatile in the next three months.

SOLAR INGRESS INTO ARIES

4/14/1999 2:00 (EDT) WASHINGTON D.C.

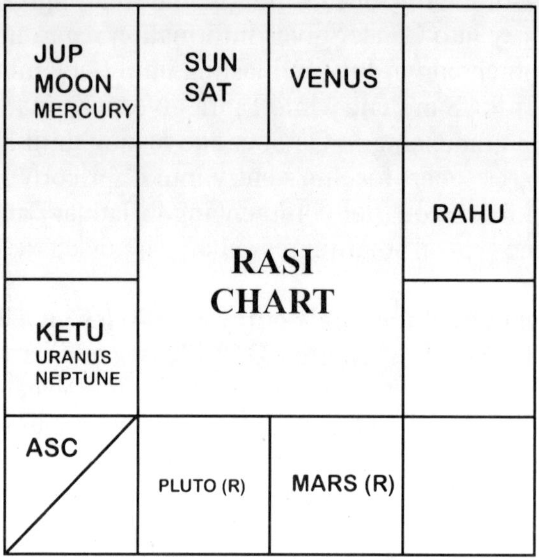

SIDEREAL LONGITUDES	
PLANET	**DEGREES IN SIGN**
ASCENDANT	♐ 20° - 10'
SUN	♈ 0° - 0'
MOON	♓ 3° - 16'
MARS (R)	♎ 13° - 56'
MERCURY	♓ 2° - 38'
JUPITER	♓ 20° - 22'
VENUS (R)	♉ 8° - 08'
SATURN	♈ 11° - 13'
RAHU	♋ 26° - 16'
KETU	♑ 26° - 16'
URANUS	♑ 22° - 22'
NEPTUNE	♑ 10° - 22'
PLUTO (R)	♏ 16° - 23'

Chart# 5

SOLAR INGRESS INTO CANCER

7/16/1999 16:00 (EDT) WASHINGTON D.C.

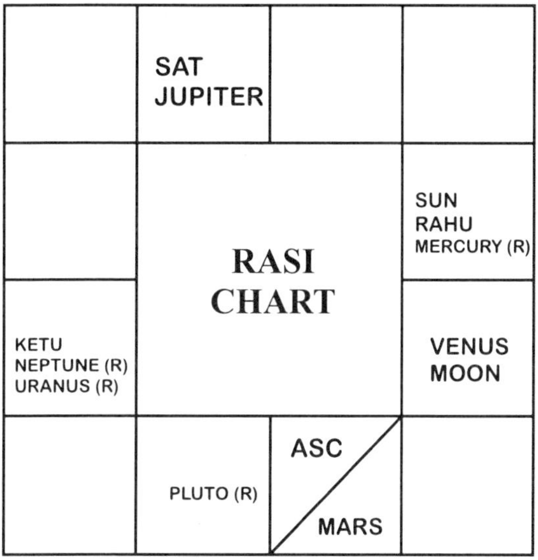

SIDEREAL LONGITUDES	
PLANET	**DEGREES IN SIGN**
ASCENDANT	♎ 29° - 52'
SUN	♋ 0° - 0'
MOON	♌ 18° - 40'
MARS	♎ 10° - 31'
MERCURY (R)	♋ 15° - 03'
JUPITER	♈ 8° - 43'
VENUS	♌ 8° - 12'
SATURN	♈ 21° - 40'
RAHU	♋ 19° - 10'
KETU	♑ 19° - 10'
URANUS (R)	♑ 21° - 48'
NEPTUNE (R)	♑ 9° - 23'
PLUTO (R)	♏ 14° - 10'

Chart # 6

DJIA numbers around this period were:

7/16/1999 -------- 11, 209.80
8/25/1999 -------- 11, 326.04
8/26/1999 -------- 11, 198.04
9/17/1999 -------- 10, 803.63.

c) Solar ingress chart for Sun's entry into Libra on 10/17/1999, 12:30 PM (EDT), Washington D.C.: Please see Chart# 7. There is a Parivarthana yoga (mutual exchange yoga) between the lord of the lagna and lord of the 5th house and also between the lord of the 9th and 11th houses from the lagna. Venus is in trine with both Jupiter and Saturn. Mercury-Sun conjunction forms a 'Raja yoga' in the 11th house. However, Rahu, Ketu, Uranus, Neptune and Pluto are adverse. It will be seen that the positive indications predominate over the negative ones. These suggest strong bullish trends in the market in the next 3 months.

DJIA numbers in this period were:

10/17/99 being a Sunday, the market was closed.
10/18/99 -------- 10, 116.28
10/28/99 -------- 10, 622.53
11/17/99 -------- 10, 884.31
12/17/99 -------- 11, 257.43

d) Solar ingress chart for Sun's entry into Capricorn on 1/14/2000 at 12:30 PM (EST), Washington DC.

Please see Chart # 8. There is a Parivarthana yoga between the lord of the lagna and lord of the 11th house. Jupiter-Saturn conjunction in the ascendant forms a Raja yoga. These are plus points. Mars which is also the lord of the 8th house is placed in the house of gains Venus, the lord of the second house is adversely placed in the 8th house along with Pluto. Rahu and Ketu are also adversely placed. Moon, the lord of the 4th house is also afflicted by Saturn. These are minus points which appear to predominate over the plus points. These indicate volatile conditions with a predominant down trend in the market in the next 3 months.

SOLAR INGRESS INTO LIBRA

10/17/1999 12:30 (EDT) WASHINGTON D.C.

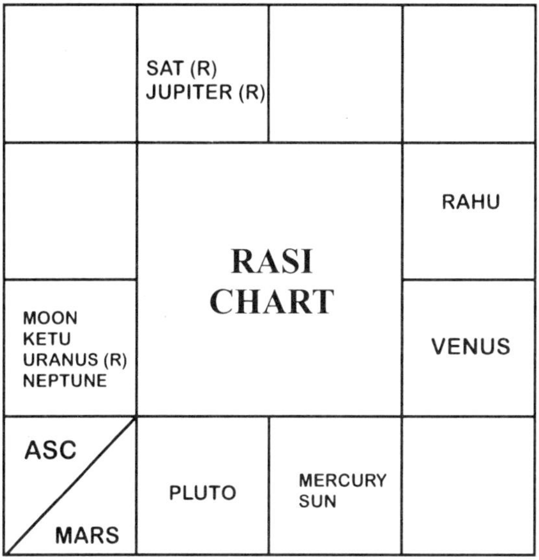

SIDEREAL LONGITUDES	
PLANET	DEGREES IN SIGN
ASCENDANT	♐ 2° - 16'
SUN	♎ 0° - 0'
MOON	♑ 0° - 42'
MARS	♐ 6° - 35'
MERCURY	♎ 23° - 08'
JUPITER (R)	♈ 6° - 53'
VENUS	♌ 14° - 14'
SATURN (R)	♈ 21° - 23'
RAHU	♋ 15° - 57'
KETU	♑ 15° - 57'
URANUS (R)	♑ 19° - 01'
NEPTUNE	♑ 7° - 44'
PLUTO	♏ 14° - 49'

Chart # 7

SOLAR INGRESS INTO CAPRICORN

1/14/2000 12:30 (EST) WASHINGTON D.C.

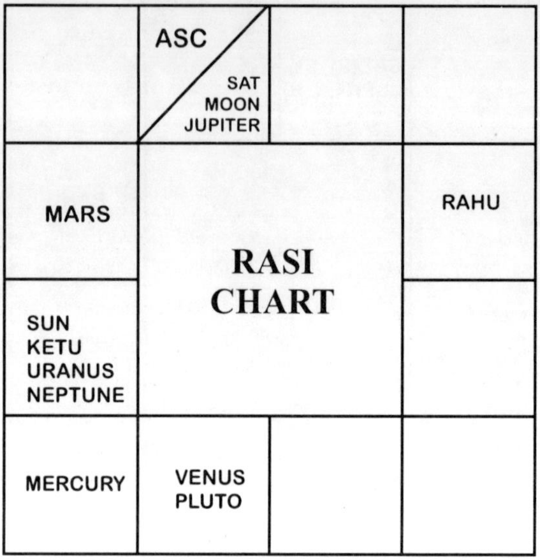

SIDEREAL LONGITUDES	
PLANET	**DEGREES IN SIGN**
ASCENDANT	♈ 21° - 17'
SUN	♑ 0° - 0'
MOON	♈ 2° - 04'
MARS	♒ 14° - 21'
MERCURY	♐ 29° - 09'
JUPITER	♈ 2° - 13'
VENUS	♏ 23° - 47'
SATURN	♈ 16° - 26'
RAHU	♋ 9° - 52'
KETU	♑ 9° - 52'
URANUS	♑ 21° - 39'
NEPTUNE	♑ 9° - 49'
PLUTO	♏ 18° - 02'

Chart # 8

DJIA numbers in the period were.
1/14/2000 -------- 11, 722.98
1/28/2000 -------- 11, 028.02
2/14/2000 -------- 10, 519.84
3/14/2000 -------- 9, 811.24

Lunation Chart for the lunation in the sign of Pisces: These charts are made for the exact moment of lunation for the capital city of a country. This chart gives information on the economy and other mundane matters concerning that country for the next 12 months followingthe month of lunation. This has been traditionally followed in India from time immemorial and has also stood the test of times. These charts are to be evaluated in the same manner as outlined above for the evaluation of the eclipse charts. Some typical lunation charts for lunation in the Sign of Pisces are given below.

1) Lunation in the sign of Pisces on 3/17/1999 at 13:30 (EST), Washington DC.: Please see Chart# 9. This chart has all the planets occupying either a quadrant or trine from the ascendant. Furthermore, the lord of the 9th house Jupiter is placed in his own sign along with Moon, Sun and Mercury. In addition, the lunation has taken place in the 9th house. Mercury is retrograde and also in trine with Pluto. Uranus, Neptune and Pluto are all in direct motion. These are plus points. Venus-Saturn conjunction is a minus point. Mars-Saturn opposition is also a minus point. All these indicate strong bullish trends in the months ahead.

DJIA numbers around the date of lunation were:

3/17/1999 -------- 9, 879.13
4/22/1999 -------- 10, 727.18
5/11/1999 -------- 11, 026.15

Lunation in the Sign of Pisces on 4/4/2000, at 14:00 (EDT), at Washington, D.C.: Please see chart # 10. It will be seen that this chart has "Kala Sarpa Yoga", which means that all the planets are hemmed in between Rahu and Ketu (outer planets not being

LUNATION IN THE SIGN PISCES

3/17/1999 13:49 (EST) WASHINGTON D.C.

SUN MOON MERCURY (R) JUPITER	VENUS SAT		
	RASI CHART		ASC RAHU
KETU URANUS NEPTUNE			
	PLUTO (R)	MARS	

SIDEREAL LONGITUDES	
PLANET	DEGREES IN SIGN
ASCENDANT	♋ 10^0 - 17'
SUN	♓ 2^0 - 53'
MOON	♓ 2^0 - 53'
MARS	♎ 18^0 - 21'
MERCURY (R)	♓ 6^0 - 40'
JUPITER	♓ 13^0 - 44'
VENUS	♈ 5^0 - 23'
SATURN	♈ 7^0 - 55'
RAHU	♋ 27^0 - 56'
KETU	♑ 27^0 - 56'
URANUS	♑ 21^0- 18'
NEPTUNE	♑ 9 -^{0}51'
PLUTO (R)	♏ 16^0- 38'

Chart # 9

LUNATION IN THE SIGN PISCES

4/4/2000 14:13 (EDT) WASHINGTON D.C.

SUN MOON VENUS	SAT MARS JUPITER		
MERCURY	RASI CHART		ASC / RAHU
KETU URANUS NEPTUNE			
	PLUTO (R)		

SIDEREAL LONGITUDES	
PLANET	DEGREES IN SIGN
ASCENDANT	♋ 17° - 48'
SUN	♓ 21° - 25'
MOON	♓ 21° - 25'
MARS	♈ 15° - 25'
MERCURY	♒ 24° - 39'
JUPITER	♓ 16° - 10'
VENUS	♓ 3° - 39'
SATURN	♈ 22° - 04'
RAHU	♋ 6° - 49'
KETU	♑ 6° - 49'
URANUS	♑ 25° - 57'
NEPTUNE	♑ 12° - 24'
PLUTO (R)	♏ 18° - 55'

Chart # 10

considered). Further, the ascendant, ascendant lord Moon and lord of the 9th house (Jupiter) are afflicted. Saturn-Mars conjunction in the 10th house is a strong negative indication. Venus in trine with Pluto is also a negative indication. Furthermore, Pluto is in retrogression. These are all minus points. However, Moon-Venus conjunction in the 9th house is causing Raja Yoga. Jupiter, Saturn and Mars combination in the 10th house also causes Raja Yoga. All these points suggest that the market is like to be volatile with a predominant downturn in the months ahead. DJIA numbers around the date of lunation were:

4/4/2000 -------- 11, 164.84
5/4/2000 -------- 10, 412.49
7/6/2000 -------- 10, 481.47
7/7/2000 -------- 10, 635.98
8/4/2000 -------- 10, 767.75

Lunation charts for the Lunation that occurs in every Zodiacal Sign.

We can make lunation charts for the lunation which occurs every month in a different zodiacal signs. This chart will indicate the trends that are likely in the following month for the corresponding chart.

Evaluation of Lunation Charts: One quick way to evaluate the lunation charts is to look for lunation itself and to see in which house from the ascendant of this chart the lunation is posited. This gives a fairly good clue to the trend in the following month. In general, it can be stated that the placement of lunation in any house duly aspected by benefic (or if benefic are placed in that house), bullish trends are indicated ahead. Conversely, for the placement of lunation in any house duly aspected by malefic (or malefics are placed in the same house), it may be stated that bearish trends are indicated ahead.
All the principles stated above in regard to the evaluation of eclipse charts do equally apply for the evaluation of the lunation charts.

Typical analysis of a lunation chart: Lunation on July 23,1998 at 9:50AM, at Washington DC.: Please see Chart # 11. The lunation has taken place in the 12th house. "Kala Sarpa Yoga" is present in this chart (outer planets not being considered). Jupiter, Uranus, Neptune, Pluto are in retrograde. Venus is conjunct with Mars. Jupiter is also retrograde. Mercury is in trine with Saturn. The above are minus points which indicate strong bearish trends ahead. DJIA numbers around the lunation day are:

7/21/1998 -------- 9, 190.20
7/22/1998 -------- 9, 128.90
7/23/1998 -------- 8, 937

Lunation on November 18, 1998 at 23:24:(EST) at Washington, D.C.: Please see Chart # 12. Lunation has taken place in the fourth house along with two benefics. Saturn is retrograde. These are minus points. Venus, Mercury are in conjunction with Pluto, which is also a minus point. This indicates volatile trends ahead. DJIA around the lunation date were:

11/19/1998 -------- 9, 039.52
11/20/1998 -------- 9, 142.82
11/23/1998 -------- 9, 357.54
12/21/1998 -------- 8, 988.25

Evaluation based on planet Mercury: The planet Mercury has a marked effect on the stock markets. Whenever Mercury becomes retrograde the market becomes either volatile or becomes bearish. Similar effects are noticed when Mercury becomes combust. The market is likely to get bullish when Mercury conjuncts with Rahu or is in trine with Rahu. The markets are likely to get bearish when Mercury conjuncts or trines Ketu. It is also observed that when Mercury changes signs in the Navamsa charts, there is a fluctuation in the stock markets. These are discussed below, under the heading, "Evaluation based on Navamsa Charts".
To make these points clear, some trinal aspects with Mercury from Rahu and Ketu are discussed below with the corresponding DJIA

LUNATION IN CANCER

7/23/1998 9:50 (EDT) WASHINGTON D.C.

JUP (R)	SAT		VENUS MARS
KETU	RASI CHART		SUN MOON
URANUS (R) NEPTUNE (R)			ASC RAHU MERCURY
	PLUTO (R)		

SIDEREAL LONGITUDES	
PLANET	**DEGREES IN SIGN**
ASCENDANT	♌ 21° - 18’
SUN	♋ 6° - 40’
MOON	♋ 6° - 44’
MARS	♊ 17° - 41’
MERCURY	♌ 2° - 10’
JUPITER (R)	♓ 4° - 10’
VENUS	♊ 10° - 54’
SATURN	♈ 9° - 19’
RAHU	♌ 7° - 50’
KETU	♒ 7° - 50’
URANUS (R)	♑ 17° - 21’
NEPTUNE (R)	♑ 6° - 57’
PLUTO (R)	♏ 11° - 36’

Chart # 11

LUNATION ON

11/18/1998 23:26 (EST) WASHINGTON D.C.

	SAT (R)		
JUPITER KETU	RASI CHART		
URANUS NEPTUNE			ASC RAHU
	MERCURY VENUS MOON SUN PLUTO		MARS

SIDEREAL LONGITUDES	
PLANET	DEGREES IN SIGN
ASCENDANT	♌ 2° - 01’
SUN	♏ 2° - 47’
MOON	♏ 2° - 47’
MARS	♍ 1° - 29’
MERCURY	♏ 23° - 19’
JUPITER	♒ 24° - 22’
VENUS	♏ 7° - 48’
SATURN (R)	♈ 4° - 20’
RAHU	♌ 2° - 58’
KETU	♒ 2° - 58’
URANUS	♑ 15°- 23’
NEPTUNE	♑ 5 -°57’
PLUTO	♏ 13°- 38’

Chart # 12

numbers that were operative at that point of time.

When Mercury conjuncts or trines Uranus, bullish conditions are likely. When Mercury conjuncts Neptune or Pluto or when Mercury trines Neptune or Pluto, bearish conditions are likely in the market.

Mercury was retrograde from 11/6/1999 to 11/24/1999. DJIA numbers in this period were:

11/5/1999 -------- 10, 704.48
11/9/1999 -------- 10, 617.32
11/12/1999 -------- 10, 770
11/24/1999 -------- 11, 024.61

Mercury was combust from 1/1/2000 to 1/31/2000. The DJIA numbers in this period were:

12/31/1999 -------- 10, 704.48
1/3/2000 -------- 11, 357
1/4/2000 -------- 10, 997
1/20/2000 -------- 11, 351.30

Mercury was sign wise in trine with Rahu from 12/7/1999 to 12/26/1999. DJIA numbers in this period were:

12/7/1999 --------- 11, 106
12/27/1999 --------- 11, 391.8
12/28/1999 --------- 11, 476.71

Mercury was sign wise in trine with Ketu in the period 12/20/2000 to 1/6/2001. DJIA numbers in this period were:

12/28/2000 -------- 10, 868.76
12/29/2000 -------- 10, 786.85
1/8/2001 -------- 10, 621.35

Evaluation based on planet Venus: The planets Venus and Mercury move very close to the Sun. Mercury does not move more than 28 degrees away from Sun; Venus does not move more than 48 degrees away from the Sun. Thus, the maximum distance between Mercury and Venus cannot be more than $28+48 = 76^0$. It is observed that whenever Mercury is farthest away from Venus, the stock market is bullish and whenever Mercury and Venus conjunct on the same degree, the stock markets become very volatile.

This is because either Mercury or Venus is likely to be in retrograde motion at that point of time.

This phenomenon which keeps repeating often helps to understand short-term trends in the stock market. To make these points clear, given below are the days when Mercury and Venus were farther apart and the corresponding DJIA numbers that were operative at that point of time. Also presented are the DJIA numbers for the days when Venus and Mercury were conjunct.

Venus had separated to the maximum extent from Mercury on 11/24/2000. DJIA numbers around this date were:
11/15/2000 -------- 10, 761.33
11/18/2000 -------- 11, 034.41
11/24/2000 -------- 11, 024.08
11/29/2000 -------- 10, 947.92

On 4/9/2001 both Venus and Mercury were conjunct on the same longitude (Venus being in retrogression). The DJIA numbers around these dates were:

4/3/2001 -------- 9, 485.71
4/5/2001 -------- 9, 918.05
4/6/2001 -------- 9, 791.09
4/9/2001 -------- 9, 845.15
4/10/2001 ------- 10, 102.74
4/11/2001 -------- 10, 013.47

Evaluation based on the Navamsa charts: In Vedic Astrology, the Navamsa chart plays a vital part in analyzing any natal chart for predictive purposes. The navamsa chart holds the key in many cases. By studying the day-to-day position of transiting planets we can infer to some extent the stock market trends. As the readers are aware, each navamsa is 3 degrees and 20 minutes in longitude. As the transiting planets move in their orbit they change the navamsa signs every 3degrees and 20 minutes. If we closely observe the navamsa position of the planets, particularly the fast moving planets like Mercury and Venus, we can get good clues regarding market behavior pattern. The principles are:.

For each sign there are 9 navamsas. As the planets transit each navamsa it becomes either bullish or bearish.
Although the principles stated below apply strictly to the behavior of commodity markets, experience has shown that the stock market trends can also be inferred by looking into navamsa position of the various transiting planets on any particular day. It is commonly observed that when the Planet Mercury changes signs in the navamsa chart there is some change in the stock market. If we closely note the navamsa concerned being transited on any particular day we are likely to have a fairly good idea of the stock market trends on that day.

The effects of planets transiting various navamsa sign wise are given below. These apply to transiting planets on a day-to-day basis. Readers are cautioned not to apply these principles in isolation as there are likely to be other planetary conditions which may run counter to these indications. Readers are therefore advised to arrive at proper conclusions about stock market trends after assessment of the sum total effects of all the planetary situations prevailing on any particular day.

Aries Sign. When planets transit Aries:

The first navamsa transited will be Aries navamsa, which indicates a bullish trend.
The second navamsa transited will be Taurus navamsa, which indicates a bullish trend.
The third navamsa transited will be Gemini navamsa, which indicates a bearish trend.

The fourth navamsa transited, will be Cancer navamsa which indicates a bearish trend.
The fifth navamsa transited will be Leo navamsa, which indicates a bullish trend.
The sixth navamsa will be Virgo navamsa, which indicates a bearish trend.
The seventh navamsa will be Libra navamsa, which indicates a bullish trend.
The eighth navamsa will be Scorpio navamsa, which indicates a bullish trend.
The ninth navamsa will be Sagittarius navamsa, which indicates a bearish trend.

Taurus Sign. When planets transit the Taurus:

The first navamsa transited will be Capricorn navamsa, which indicates a bullish trend.
The second navamsa transited will be Aquarius navamsa, which indicates a bullish trend.
The third navamsa transited will be Pisces navamsa, which indicates a bearish trend.
The fourth navamsa transited will be Aries navamsa, which indicates a bullish trend.
The fifth navamsa transited will be Taurus navamsa, which indicates a bullish trend.
The sixth navamsa transited will be Gemini navamsa, which indicates a bearish trend.
The seventh navamsa transited will be Cancer navamsa, which indicates a bullish trend.
The eighth navamsa transited will be Leo navamsa, which indicates a bullish trend.
The ninth navamsa transited, will be Virgo navamsa, which indicates a bearish trend.

Gemini sign: When planets transit Gemini:

The first navamsa transited will be Libra navamsa, which indicates a bullish trend.

The second navamsa transited will be Scorpio navamsa, which indicates a bullish trend.
The third navamsa transited will be Sagittarius, which indicates a bearish trend.
The fourth navamsa transited will be Capricorn navamsa, which indicates a bullish trend.
The fifth navamsa transited will be Aquarius navamsa, which indicates a bullish trend.
The sixth navamsa transited will be Pisces navamsa, which indicates a bearish trend.
The seventh navamsa transited will be Aries navamsa, which indicates a bullish trend.
The eighth navamsa transited will be Taurus navamsa, which indicates a bullish trend.
The ninth navamsa transited will be Gemini navamsa, which indicates a bearish trend.

Cancer Sign: When planets transit Cancer:

The first navamsa transited will be Cancer navamsa, which indicates a bullish trend.
The second navamsa transited will be Leo navamsa, which indicates a bullish trend.
The third navamsa transited will be Virgo navamsa, which indicates a bearish trend.
The fourth navamsa transited will be Libra navamsa, which indicates a bullish trend.
The fifth navamsa transited will be Scorpio navamsa, which indicates a bullish trend.
The sixth navamsa transited will be Sagittarius navamsa, which indicates a bearish trend.
The seventh navamsa transited will be Capricorn navamsa, which indicates a bullish trend.
The eighth navamsa transited will be Aquarius navamsa, which indicates a bullish trend.
The ninth navamsa transited will be Pisces navamsa, which indicates a bearish trend.

Leo sign. When planets transit Leo:

The first navamsa transited will be Aries navamsa, which indicates a bullish trend.
The second navamsa transited will be Taurus navamsa, which indicates a bullish trend.
The third navamsa transited will be Gemini navamsa, which indicates a bearish trend.
The fourth navamsa transited will be Cancer navamsa, which indicates a bullish trend.
The fifth navamsa transited will be Leo navamsa, which indicates a bullish trend.
The sixth navamsa transited, will be Virgo navamsa, which indicates a bearish trend.
The seventh navamsa transited will be Libra navamsa, which indicates a bullish trend.
The eighth navamsa transited will be Scorpio navamsa, which indicates bullish trend.
The ninth navamsa transited will be Sagittarius navamsa, which indicates a bearish trend.

Virgo Sign: When planets transit Virgo:

The first navamsa transited will be Capricorn navamsa, which indicates a bullish trend.
The second navamsa transited will be Aquarius navamsa, which indicates a bullish trend.
The third navamsa transited will be Pisces navamsa, which indicates a bearish trend.
The fourth navamsa transited will be Aries navamsa, which indicates a bullish trend.
The fifth navamsa transited will be Taurus navamsa which indicates a bullish trend.
The sixth navamsa transited will be Gemini navamsa which indicates a bearish trend.
The seventh navamsa transited will be Cancer navamsa which indicates a bullish trend.
The eighth navamsa transited will be Leo navamsa which indicates a bullish trend.

The ninth navamsa transited will be Virgo navamsa
which indicates a bearish trend.

Libra sign: When planets transit the Libra sign:

The first navamsa transited will be Libra navamsa
which indicates a bullish trend.
The second navamsa transited will be scorpio navamsa
which indicates a bullish trend.
The third navamsa transited will be Sagittarius navamsa
which indicates a bearish trend.
The fourth navamsa transited will be Capricorn navamsa,
which indicates a bullish trend.
The fifth navamsa transited will be Aquarius navamsa,
which indicates a bullish trend.
The sixth navamsa transited will be Pisces navamsa,
which indicates a bearish trend.
The seventh navamsa transited will be Aries navamsa,
which indicates a bullish trend.
The eighth navamsa transited will be Taurus navamsa,
which indicates a bullish trend.
The ninth navamsa transited will be Gemini navamsa,
which indicates a bearish trend.

Scorpio Sign: When planets transit Scorpio:

The first navamsa transited will be Cancer navamsa,
which indicates a bullish trend.
The second navamsa transited will be Leo navamsa,
which indicates a bullish trend.
The third navamsa transited will be Virgo navamsa,
which indicates a bearish trend.
The fourth navamsa transited will be Libra navamsa,
which indicates a bullish trend.
The fifth navamsa transited will be Scorpio navammsa,
which indicates a bullish trend.
The sixth navamsa transited will be Sagittarius navamsa,
which indicates a bearish trend.

The seventh navamsa transited will be Capricorn navamsa, which indicates a bullish trend.
The eighth navamsa transited will be Aquarius navamsa, which indicates a bullish trend.
The ninth navamsa transited will be Pisces navamsa, which indicates a bearish trend.

Sagittarius Sign: When planets transit Sagittarius:

The first navamsa transited will be Aries navamsa, which indicates a bullish trend.
The second navamsa transited will be Taurus navamsa, which indicates a bullish trend.
The third navamsa transited will be Gemini navamsa, which indicates a bearish trend.
The fourth navamsa transited will be Cancer navamsa, which indicates a bullish trend.
The fifth navamsa transited will be Leo navamsa, which indicates a bullish trend.
The sixth navamsa transited will be Virgo navamsa, which indicates a bearish trend.
The seventh navamsa transited will be Libra navamsa, which indicates a bullish trend.

The eighth navamsa transited will be Scorpio navamsa, which indicates a bullish trend.
The ninth navamsa transited will be a Sagittarius navamsa, which indicates a bearish trend.

Capricorn Sign: When planets transit Capricorn:

The first navamsa transited will be Capricorn navamsa, which indicates a bullish trend.
The second navamsa transited will be Aquarius navamsa, which indicates a bullish trend.
The third navamsa transited will be Pisces navamsa, which indicates a bearish trend.
The fourth navamsa transited will be Aries navamsa which indicates a bullish trend.

The fifth navamsa transited will be Taurus navamsa which indicates a bullish trend.
The sixth navamsa transited will be Gemini navamsa which indicates a bearish trend.
The seventh navamsa transited will be Cancer navamsa which indicates a bullish trend.
The eighth navamsa transited will be Leo navamsa which indicates a bullish trend.
The ninth navamsa transited will be Virgo navamsa which indicates a bearish trend.

Aquarius Sign: When planets transit Aquarius:

The first navamsa transited will be Libra navamsa which indicates a bullish trend.
The second navamsa transited will be Scorpio navamsa which indicates a bullish trend.
The third navamsa transited will be Sagittarius navamsa which indicates a bearish trend.
The fourth navamsa transited will be Capricorn navamsa which indicates a bullish trend.
The fifth navamsa transited will be Aquarius navamsa which indicates a bullish trend.
The sixth navamsa transited will be Pisces navamsa which indicates a bearish trend.
The seventh navamsa transited will be Aries navamsa which indicates a bullish trend.
The eighth navamsa transited will be Taurus navamsa which indicates a bullish trend.
The ninth navamsa will be Gemini navamsa which l indicates a bearish trend.

Pisces Sign: When planets transit Pisces:

The first navamsa transited will be Cancer navamsa which indicates a bullish trend.
The second navamsa transited will be Leo navamsa which indicates a bearish trend.
The third navamsa transited will be Virgo navamsa which will indicate a bearish trend.

The fourth navamsa transited will Libra navamsa which indicates a bullish trend.
The fifth navamsa transited will be Scorpio navamsa which indicates a bullish trend.
The sixth navamsa transited will be Sagittarius navamsa which indicates a bearish trend.
The seventh navamsa transited will be Capricorn navamsa which indicates a bullish trend.
The eighth navamsa transited will be Aquarius navamsa which indicates a bullish trend.
The ninth navamsa transited will be Pisces navamsa which indicates a bearish trend.

Evaluation based on Ashtaka Varga chart of the New York Stock Exchange: Readers who have some basic knowledge of the ashtaka varga system of prediction will be able to appreciate this method of evaluation of stock market trends. This method is based on the principle that whenever planets transit high bindus (points) in their respective Binnashtaka varga charts they tend to give favorable results and whenever they transit low bindus (points) in their respective Binashtakavarga charts they tend to give adverse results. The author had applied these principles in evaluating the market trends with a fair degree of success. Readers are cautioned to use this method after they get very familiar with the basic principles of Ashtaka Varga. In this method, a Vedic Astrological chart is made out for the New York Stock Exchange based on the date of the inauguration, namely, 5/17/1792 at 8:52 AM at New York, New York (Ref: "Financial Astrology", by LCdr. David Williams). Please see Chart# 13.

Based on the chart of NYSE, a Binnashtaka varga chart is prepared for the planets Mercury and Venus. The reason being that both Mercury and Venus specifically appear to influence the market trends in the short term.

The Binnashtaka varga chart made out for the planets Mercury and Venus may (Please see Charts # 14 and # 15) It will be seen from the binnashtaka varga chart of Mercury that Mercury has low bindus (3 bindus or points) in the sign scorpio and that Mercury has the high bindus (7 bindus) in Aries. Therefore,

NEW YORK STOCK EXCHANGE INAUGURATION
5/17/1792 8:52 (EST) NEW YORK, NY.

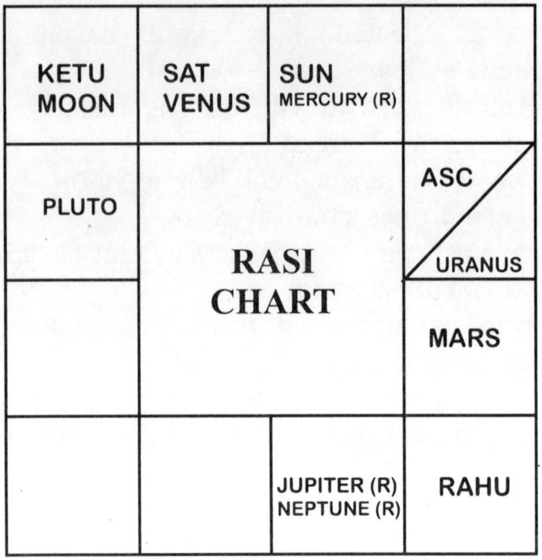

SIDEREAL LONGITUDES	
PLANET	DEGREES IN SIGN
ASCENDANT	♋ 6° - 03’
SUN	♉ 6° - 16’
MOON	♓ 28° - 14’
MARS	♌ 27° - 46’
MERCURY (R)	♉ 2° - 50’
JUPITER (R)	♎ 1° - 59’
VENUS	♈ 14° - 28’
SATURN	♈ 5° - 24’
RAHU	♍ 11° - 15’
KETU	♓ 11° - 15’
URANUS	♋ 24°- 11’
NEPTUNE (R)	♎ 6 -°44’
PLUTO	♒ 2 -°33’

Chart # 13

NEW YORK STOCK EXCHANGE

4	7	6	3
5			ASC 4
4			5
4	3	5	4

BINNASHTAKA VARGA CHART OF MERCURY

Chart # 14

NEW YORK STOCK EXCHANGE

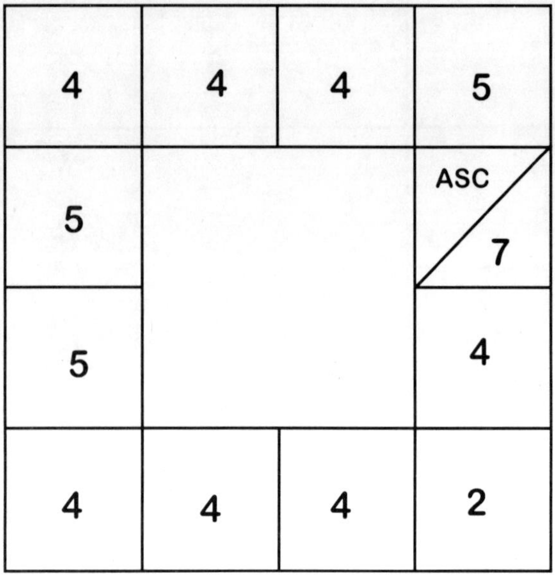

**BINNASHTAKA VARGA
CHART OF
VENUS**

Chart # 15

whenever Mercury transits Scorpio having low bindus, the market is likely to have downturn and thus it will present a buying opportunity. Whenever Mercury transits Aries with high bindus, the market is likely to have upturns and thus will present a selling opportunity. Similarly, taking the Binnashtaka varga chart of Venus it is seen that it has lowest bindus (2 bindus) in Virgo and highest bindus (7 bindus) in Cancer. Whenever Venus transits Virgo the market is likely to have a downturn and whenever Venus transits Cancer the market is likely to have upturns.

It will be seen from the binnashtaka varga chart of Mercury that Aries has 7 bindus and Taurus has 6 bindus. Mercury has low bindus in Gemini(3 bindus) and Scorpio (3 bindus).

It will be seen from the Binnashtaka varga chart of Venus that Cancer has 7 bindus and Virgo has the lowest bindus (just 2 bindus). Whenever Mercury transits Taurus and if simultaneously Venus transits Cancer, the market is likely to have a bullish trend.

From June 1,1999 to June 4,1999 Mercury transited Taurus (7 bindus) and simultaneously Venus transited cancer (7 bindus). Both Mercury and Venus were in direct motion in this period. But Mars, Uranus, Neptune and Pluto were in retrograde motion The DJIA numbers in this period were:

6/1//1999 -------- 10,596.26
6/2/1999 -------- 10,577.89
6/3/1999 ------- 10,663.69
6/4/1999 -------- 10,799.84

Whenever Mercury transits a sign with low bindus and simultaneously if Venus also transits a sign having low bindus, the market is likely to have a bearish trend. From November 4, 1999 to November 15, 1999 Mercury was in Scorpio(3 bindus) and simultaneously Venus was in Virgo (2 bindus). Mercury in this period was in direct motion until 11/5/99 and then became retrograde; and while in retrogression it entered Libra on 11/16/99.

The DJIA numbers in this period were:

11/4/1999 -------- 10, 639.64
11/5/1999 -------- 10, 704.48
11/6/1999 -------- Saturday, Market closed.
11/7/1999 -------- Sunday, Market closed.
11/8/1999 -------- 10, 718.85
11/9/1999 -------- 10, 617.32
11/10/1999 -------- 10, 597.74
11/11/1999 -------- 10, 595.30
11/12/1999 -------- 10, 770.54
11/13/1999 -------- Saturday, Market closed.
11/14/1999 -------- Sunday, Market closed.
11/15/1999 -------- 10, 761.37
11/16/1999 -------- 10, 932.33 (* Mercury while in retrogression entered Libra having 5 bindus on this day).

Readers are cautioned not to apply this principle in isolation. It is observed that other factors like retrogression of planets, direct motion of planets and planetary aspects of benefics and malefics try to influence the Market trends in addition to the above.

From July 9, 2000 to July 31, 2000, Mercury transited Gemini having 3 bindus and simultaneously Venus transited Cancer having 7 bindus. However in this period Mercury which was initially retrograde became direct from July 17 onwards while Venus was in direct motion in this period.. In this period, Uranus, Neptune and Pluto were also retrograde.
The DJIA numbers in this period were:

7/6/2000 ------- 10, 481.47 (*Mercury was already in retrograde motion on this day).
7/7/2000 --------10, 635.98
7/9/2000 --------Sunday, Market closed.
7/10/2000 -------- 10, 646.58
7/11/2000 -------- 10, 727.19
7/12/2000 -------- 10, 783.76
7/13/2000 -------- 10, 788.71
7/14/2000 -------- 10, 812.75

7/17/2000 -------- 10, 804.27 (* Mercury was direct from this day).
7/18/2000 -------- 10, 739.92
7/19/2000 -------- 10, 696.08
7/20/2000 -------- 10, 843.81
7/21/2000 -------- 10, 733.56
7/22/2000 -------- Saturday ---Market closed.
7/23/2000 -------- Sunday---Market closed.
7/24/2000 -------- 10, 685.12
7/25/1999 -------- 10, 699.97
7/26/1999 -------- 10, 516.48
7/27/1999 -------- 10, 586.17
7/28/1999 -------- 10, 411.17
7/29/1999 -------- SaturdayMarket closed.
7/30/1999 -------- Sunday Market closed.
7/31/1999 --------10, 521.98

From September 9, 2000 to September 23, 2000, Mercury was in Virgo having 4 bindus and Venus was also simultaneously in Virgo having 2 bindus. Both Mercury as well as Venus were in direct motion. But Uranus, Neptune and Pluto were in retrograde motion in this period and Saturn was in retrograde motion from 9/13/2000 onwards. Venus entered Libra (having 4 bindus) on 9/20/2000. The DJIA numbers in this period were:

9/9/2000 & 9/10/2000 Saturday & Sunday - Marketclosed.
9/11/2000 -------- 11, 195.49
9/12/2000 -------- 11, 233.27
9/13/2000 -------- 11, 182.18
9/14/2000 -------- 11, 087.47
9/15/2000 --------10, 927.00
9/16/2000 & 9/17/2000 (Saturday & Sunday - Market closed).
9/18/2000 -------- 10, 808.52
9/19/2000 -------- 10, 789.29
9/20/2000 -------- 10, 687.92 (* Venus enters Libra).
9/21/2000 -------- 10, 765.52
9/22/2000 -------- 10, 812.32

The points made above indicate that Ashtakavarga charts also serve as one of the tools to predict the stock market trends.

Evaluation based on "Panchak" Phenomenon: As already explained the 'Panchak' phenomenon takes place every month on a 27-day cycle. This happens whenever Moon transits the five consecutive nakshatras in the signs of Aquarius and Pisces namely, Dhanishta -2nd and -3rd padas, Satabisha, Poorvabhadrapada, Uttarabhadrapada and Revathi.
The 'panchak' phenomenon lasts for 5 days and repeats itself on a 27day cycle.

The following are the effects of 'panchak' generally observed in relation to stock markets.

1) If the first half of 'panchak' period is bullish then the second half of 'panchak' period is likely to be bearish.

2) If the first half of 'panchak' period is bearish then the second half of 'panchak' period is likely to be bullish.

3) If 'panchak' period commences on a Tuesday or Saturday or Sunday then the 'panchak' period is likely to be bullish.

4) If the 'panchak' period commences on a Monday or Wednesday or Thursday or Friday then the 'panchak' period is likely to be bearish.

Readers are cautioned not to take these principles in isolation and apply them to the stock markets.

The actual behavior of the market will depend on the effects of the planetary situation on any day. As such, the 'panchak' can be used as a rough guide to understand the trends that are likely during the duration of the 'panchak' phenomenon.

It is advised that proper conclusions should be drawn after taking into considerations situation of all the transiting planets on the day concerned. The points made above will be better understood from the following. Here, the various 'panchak' periods that occurred in the recent past are discussed with the DJIA that prevailed at that point of time. This will help the readers to form their own conclusions in regard to future 'panchak' period.

'Panchak' was on from 3/3/2000 to 3/8/2000.

3/3/2000 was a Friday. As per the above, this was conducive to a bearish trend in the market.

On 3/3/2000 DJIA was 10, 363.79 (up from previous close by 198.37).
Market was closed on 3/4/2000 and 3/5/2000. On 3/6/2000 DJIA was 10, 170.50 (down 196.70 from previous day's close).

'Panchak' was on from 9/11/2000 to 9/15/2000.

9/11/2000 was a Monday. As per the above, this is conducive to bearish trends in the market.
On 9/11/2000 DJIA was 11, 195.49(down 25.16 from previous day's close).
On 9/12/2000 DJIA was 11, 233.27 (up by 37.74 from previous day's close).
On 9/13/2000 DJIA was 11, 182.18 (down 51.05 from previous days close.
On 9/14/2000 DJIA was 11, 087.47 (down 94.71 from previous day's close).
ON 9/15/2000 DJIA was 10, 927.00 (down 160.47 from previous day's close).
On 3/7/2000 DJIA was 9, 796.03 (down 374.47 from previous day's close).
On 3/8/2000 DJIA was 9, 856.53 (up by 49.42 from previous day's close).

'Panchak' was on from 9/11/2000 to 9/15/2000.

9/11/2000 was a Monday. As per the above this was conducive to bearish trends in the market.
On 9/11/2000 DJIA was 11, 195.49 (down 25.16 from previous day's close).
On 9/12/2000 DJIA was 11, 233.27 (up by 37.74 from previous day's close).
On 9/13/2000 DJIA was 11, 182.18 (down 51.05 from previous days close).

On 9/14/2000 DJIA was 11, 087.47
(down 94.71 from previous day's close).
ON 9/15/2000 DJIA was 10, 927.00 (down 160.47 from previous day's close).

'Panchak' was on from 4/17/2001 to 4/21/2001.

4/17/2001 was a Tuesday. As per the above this was conducive to bullish trends in the market.
On 4/17/2001 DJIA was 10, 204.56 (up by 46.01 from previous day's close).
On 4/18/2001 DJIA was 10, 615.83 (up by 399.10 from previous day's close)
On 4/19/2001 DJIA was 10, 693.71 (up 77.88 from previous day's close)
On 4/20/2001 DJIA was 10, 579.85 (down 113.86 from previous day's close).
4/21/2001 being a Saturday, the market was closed.

6) How to evaluate long term trends based on the chart for the New York Stock Exchange.

New York stock exchange was formally inaugurated on 5/17/1792 at 8:52AM at New York, New York (Ref: Financial Astrology by L.Cdr. David Williams). The Sidereal chart made for this date, time and place of inauguration may be seen at Chart # 10.
The progressed Major Dasas since the very inception are:

Mercury Dasa from 5/17/1792 to 8/15/1794
Ketu Dasa from 8/15/1794 to 8/15/1801
Venus Dasa from 8/15/1801 to 8/15/1821
Sun Dasa from 8/15/1821 to 8/15/1827
Moon Dasa from 8/15/1827 to 8/15/1837
Mars Dasa from 8/15/1837 to 8/15/1844
Rahu Dasa from 8/15/1844 to 8/15/1862
Jupiter Dasa from 8/15/1862 to 8/15/1878
Saturn Dasa from 8/15/1878 to 8/15/1897
Mercury Dasa from 8/15/1897 to 8/15/1914
Ketu Dasa from 8/15/1914 to 8/15/1921
Venus Dasa from 8/15/1921 to 8/15/1941

Sun Dasa from 8/15/1941 to 8/15/1947
Moon Dasa from 8/15/1947 to 8/15/1957
Mars Dasa from 8/15/1957 to 8/15/1964

The various antar dasas in the current Saturn Dasa are:

Saturn Dasa-Saturn antar dasa from 8/15/1998 to 8/18/2001
Saturn Dasa-Mercury antar dasa from 8/18/ 2001 to 4/27/2004
Saturn Dasa-Ketu antar dasa from 4/27/2004 to 6/6/2005
Saturn Dasa-Venus antar dasa from 6/6/2005 to 8/6/2008
Saturn Dasa-Sun antar dasa from 8/6/2008 to 8/17/2009
Saturn Dasa-Moon antar dasa from 8/17/2009 to 3/17/2011
Saturn Dasa-Mars antar dasa from 3/17/2011 to 4/26/ 2012
Saturn Dasa-Rahu antar dasa from 4/26/2012 to 3/2/2015
Saturn Dasa-Jupiter antar dasa from 3/2/2015 to 9/14/2017

How does the above progressed dasas and antar dasas help evaluate long term trends in NYSE? We note from the above that the antar dasa of Mercury will commence on 8/18/2001 and will last until 4/27/2004. In the natal chart of NYSE, Mercury is posited in the 11th house from the ascendant. This means that the market trends are likely to be very positive from 8/18/2001.

7) Evaluation of Stocks of Companies and Corporations based on their Natal Sidereal Charts: We can prepare a sidereal chart of any corporation if the date, time and place of incorporation is available. In case only the date and place of incorporation are available, then also we can prepare the sidereal chart assuming the time of incorporation as 12 noon at the place of incorporation. Similarly, we can prepare a sidereal chart for even small companies provided the date and place of incorporation or date and place of commencement of business.

How to Evaluate the Fortunes of a Joint Stock Company or a Corporation: We interpret the sidereal charts of companies in the same way as we interpret the natal charts of persons by progressing the vimshottari dasa and also delineating the results based on the ashtakavarga charts. The only difference is that in the case of corporations and companies we follow the principles of mundane astrology.

Based on the principles of mundane astrology the principles to be followed in delineating the results of the various houses and planets posited therein in the sidereal charts of companies are given below.

First House gives information about the top management of the company, its shareholders and also the company's objectives as perceived by the public and the company's own standing in the market.

Second House gives information about the wealth of the company which include the cash reserves, ability to do profitable business and the financial health of the company.

Third House gives information about public relations of the company and also the dissemination of information about the company, advertisement and the demand in the market for the company's shares etc.

Fourth House gives information about the real estate holdings of the company and investments in land for office buildings, factories, factory outlets, warehouses etc.

Fifth House gives information about the entertainments and social activities of the company, conventions and seminars, the middle level management in the company and the attitude of stock holders.

Sixth House gives information about the health of the employees of the company, the labor relations and situations like strike etc. It also gives information about the debt and loans of the company.

Seventh House gives information about the competition and adversaries. It also gives information about the agreements and contracts with outside agencies.

Eighth House gives information about the gains and losses as a result of the decisions taken by the management of the company. It also gives information about the financial situations arising out of mergers, acquisition, legacies, litigations etc.

Ninth House gives information about publicity, advertisement and public relations.

Tenth House gives information about the top management of the company like CEO of the company etc. This also gives information about the standing of the company in the market place.

Eleventh House gives information about the revenues and earnings of the company and in general its financial health.

Twelfth House gives information about labor problems, strikes, employee attitudes etc. It also gives information about the secret activities and plots to disintegrate the company, research and development, gathering of trade secrets of competition etc.

Typical Chart of Corporations: The chart of Boeing Corporation is given in Chart # 16. This chart indicates good placement of planets mostly in quadrant and trinal houses. The chart of Walmart is given in Chart # 17 which indicates a good placement of planets mostly in quadrants and trinal houses.

Does the date of Incorporation Impact the fortune of a Company?

Yes. It is of common knowledge that out of the several companies incorporated, some succeed and some don't. The key to the success or failure lies in the date of corporation. Traditionally, electional astrology has been used in India from time immemorial for activities such as starting a business or forming a company. Here we choose the best date and time as applicable to the location of the company. This will ensure a good natal chart for the company having a potential for success. Experience in India has shown by and large companies incorporated on a predetermined auspicious day have good track record of success.

Readers are aware that in the Year 2000, many 'dot.com' companies that were expected to succeed actually failed. Perhaps the date of incorporation of these companies may have a clue as to why they failed.

BOEING CORPORATION

7/19/1934 13:00 (EST) DELAWARE

	URANUS		VENUS MARS MERCURY(R)
SAT (R)	**RASI CHART**		SUN KETU PLUTO
RAHU			NEPTUNE
		ASC MOON	JUP

SIDEREAL LONGITUDES	
PLANET	**DEGREES IN SIGN**
ASCENDANT	♎ 10° - 08'
SUN	♋ 3° - 24'
MOON	♎ 2° - 58'
MARS	♊ 9° - 39'
MERCURY (R)	♊ 21° - 29'
JUPITER	♍ 22° - 30'
VENUS	♊ 2° - 16'
SATURN (R)	♒ 3° - 56'
RAHU	♑ 17° - 23'
KETU	♋ 17° - 23'
URANUS	♈ 8° - 22'
NEPTUNE	♌ 17° - 33'
PLUTO	♋ 1° - 25'

Chart # 16

WALMART

10/31/1969 12:00 (EST) DOVER, DE

	SAT (R)		MOON
RAHU	RASI CHART		
MARS			KETU
ASC	NEPTUNE	SUN MERCURY	VENUS JUP URANUS PLUTO

SIDEREAL LONGITUDES	
PLANET	DEGREES IN SIGN
ASCENDANT	♐ 24° - 55'
SUN	♎ 14° - 40'
MOON	♊ 27° - 23'
MARS	♑ 3° - 39'
MERCURY	♎ 4° - 54'
JUPITER	♍ 27° - 40'
VENUS	♍ 24° - 05'
SATURN (R)	♈ 11° - 49'
RAHU	♒ 26° - 25'
KETU	♌ 26° - 25'
URANUS	♍ 13° - 02'
NEPTUNE	♏ 4° - 15'
PLUTO	♍ 3° - 0'

Chart # 17

Chapter Four

When to Buy and when to Sell Stocks.

The oft repeated mantra of the stock market is to buy the stocks when the market is 'low' and sell the stocks when the market is 'high'. In practice it is very difficult to arrive at the precise 'low' point for buying or precise 'high' point for selling. Several methods have been suggested by analysts but they are not found to be foolproof. Here the Vedic Astrology seems to have a fairly reasonable answer.

Using Vedic Astrology and using one's own natal chart and the corresponding chart of the transiting planets it is possible to determine the 'buy' and 'sell' points to a reasonable degree of accuracy. These are discussed below.

As brought out in Chapter 2 and 3, we should always keep in mind the big picture of both long term and short term trends evaluated based on the principles described in those chapters. Withing the framework of this big picture, we should fine tune the buying and selling opportunities which are described below. The natal chart should indicate a favorable maha dasa or antar dasa or pratyantar dasa on the day of entering the stock market deals. In addition, the transiting planets should also be favorable.

How to Evaluate a Good Buying Opportunity in the Stock Market.

The points made in Chapter 3 will enable the reader to evaluate both the short term and the long term trends in the market. Generally it will be wise to buy when the market is at the bottom as revealed by these trends. We can fine tune the buying opportunity further, by using the following tips.

During the favorable antar dasa or pratyantar dasa period we can fine tune the days based on the ashtaka varga chart. The days on which maximum number of planets transit kakshyas with bindu will be more favorable and conducive to success. Generally, the adverse periods in one's natal chart will not be conducive to success either for 'buying' or 'selling' and hence during such adverse period it is better to avoid either 'buying' or 'selling'.

Simultaneously, coinciding with the good period in the natal chart the transiting planets should also a present a favorable picture in regard to bearish trends in the stock markets. For example, given a good period in one's natal chart one should choose a 'time slot' in which Mercury is in trine with a malefic like Ketu or Mars; or Mercury being conjunct with a malefic or conjunct with Venus etc. The periods when Mercury is combust will also indicate change of trends in the markets. These combinations have already been discussed above. Furthermore, during the periods of retrogression of planets like Mercury, Venus and Mars the market gets into a volatile mode that is sometimes bullish and sometimes bearish. These points can be ascertained in advance by looking at the Ephemeris. Some times natal chart may not show very adverse periods but if the transiting planets indicate strong bearish trends followed by bullish trends, it will be wise to choose such time slots for a “buying” opportunity while the market is in the bearish mode.

How to Evaluate a Good Selling Opportunity in the Stock Market.

The best period to sell will be when the market is at the peak. This can be broadly evaluated for the short term and long term trends discussed in Chapter 3. We can further fine tune the buying opportunity by using the following tips.

Basically the natal chart should indicate a favorable period. During periods of favorable maha dasa, or antar dasa or pratyantar dasa in one's natal chart it is advisable to ‘sell’ and get out of the stock market. This is likely to ensure some profit or at best minimum losses. Based on ashtaka varga selling is to be done on the days when maximum number of planets transit kakshyas with bindus. On the days when the maximum number of planets transit kakshyas without a bindu one should lie low and keep a low profile and should not either buy or sell stocks.

Simultaneously, coinciding with the good period in one's natal chart one should pick up 'time slots' during which either the planet Mercury is 'direct' or in trine with Rahu and a benefic like Jupiter. When Mercury separates as far away from Venus (the maximum is 68 degrees), bullish trends are likely. Sometimes the natal charts may not have very favorable periods but if the transiting planets indicate the likelihood of strong bullish trends then also we are likely to succeed. In those cases when we choose such 'time slots' based only on the transiting planets, we are likely to sell at a higher price. To make the above points clear, some of the buying and selling opportunities that occurred in the past, based on the above principles, are given below. Reasoning is also provided for the 'buying' or 'selling' along with the DJ index that ruled on that day. Out of the several points enumerated above, we may consider the following point: Mercury trines Ketu (sign wise) gives a good buying opportunity amongst other factors and Mercury trines Rahu (sign wise) gives a good selling opportunity amongst other factors. Readers are cautioned not to use this method in isolation but they are advised to consider the effect of other transiting planets also and arrive at their own conclusions.

Buying opportunity on 1/28/2000. On this day, Mercury was in trine with ketu. The DJIA on this day was 10, 838.87.

Selling opportunity on 4/14/2000. On this day, Mercury was transiting Pisces and was in trine with Rahu posited in the sign Cancer. On this day DJIA was 11, 221.93.

Buying opportunity on 5/15/2000. On this day, Mercury was transiting Taurus, which was in trine with Ketu. Further, Mercury and Saturn were conjunct in Taurus. The DJIA on that day was 10, 807.78.

Selling opportunity on 8/10/2000. On this day, Mercury was transiting Cancer sign and was thus conjunct Rahu posited in the same sign. On this day DJIA was 10, 908.76.

Buying opportunity on 1/2/2001. On this day, Mercury was transiting Sagittarius thus in conjunct with Ketu posited in that sign. The DJIA on that day was 10, 646.15.

Selling opportunity on 5/24/2001. On this day, Mercury was transiting Gemini sign and was thus conjunct Rahu posited in that sign. The DJIA on that day was 11, 122.42.

Chapter Five

How to correlate all of the above-mentioned factors and arrive at proper conclusions.

First of all we should consider the "lunation chart" for the lunation in the sign of Pisces. In India it is believed that this chart will indicate the trends for the next 12 months. By looking at this chart we can infer the trends that are likely in the next 12 months.

Then we should consider the solar ingress chart for Sun's entry into Aries. This chart is also believed to indicate the trends for the whole year. Then we should consider if any planet is in retrogression. If eclipses occur we should consider the chart of the eclipse in that month. Then we should evaluate the solar ingress chart concerning that month. After examining the positive and negative indications in these charts we should arrive at conclusions regarding the trends that are likely to prevail in the market for that month. Based on these considerations, market trends that are likely for the years 2001 and 2002 are given below.

Market projections for the year 2001.

There are five eclipses which are due to occur in this year.

1) Total Lunar eclipse on 1/9/2001
2) Total Solar eclipse on 6/21/2001
3) Partial Lunar eclipse on 7/5/2001.
4) Annular Solar eclipse on 12/14/2001
5) Penumbral Lunar eclipse on 12/30/2001.

Transits of Major Planets:

Jupiter will transit Taurus until June 16, 2001 and from June 17 onwards it will transit Gemini. Saturn will transit Taurus throughout this year. Rahu will transit Gemini throughout this year and Ketu will transit Sagittarius throughout this year.

Uranus will transit Capricorn until April 10 and then will move over to Aquarius on April 11. Uranus will be retrograde on May 30 and reenter Capricorn on July 20 and becomes direct on October 30. It will continue to be in Capricorn for the remaining months of the year.

Neptune will transit Capricorn for the entire year. Neptune will be retrograde from May 11 until October 18, 2001, then it becomes direct.

Pluto will transit Scorpio for the entire year. Pluto will be retrograde from March 19 until August 23, 2001 then it becomes direct.

General Observations for the Year 2001:

Lunation chart for Lunation in Pisces on 3/24/2001.

Please see Chart # 18.

This chart has a major negative indication due to the adverse placement of Saturn in the 8th house in opposition to Pluto and Mars. This suggests some National calamity down the road (please refer to details under the 8th house in Page @@@.), which has the potential to impact the market with down trends.

Solar Ingress chart for Sun's entry into Aries on 4/13/2001.

Please see Chart# 19. The major negative indication in this chart is the adverse placement of Rahu in the 12th house in

LUNATION IN PISCES

3/24/2001 20:21 (EST) WASHINGTON D.C.

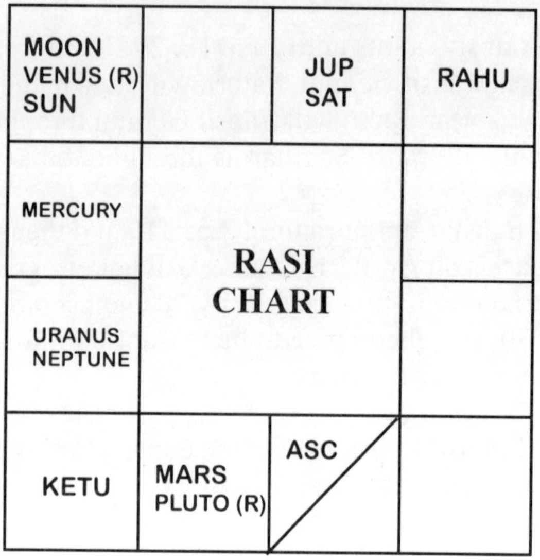

SIDEREAL LONGITUDES	
PLANET	**DEGREES IN SIGN**
ASCENDANT	♎ 4° - 54'
SUN	♓ 10° - 35'
MOON	♓ 10° - 35'
MARS	♏ 24° - 08'
MERCURY	♒ 16° - 36'
JUPITER	♉ 12° - 34'
VENUS (R)	♓ 18° - 47'
SATURN	♉ 3° - 13'
RAHU	♊ 17° - 45'
KETU	♐ 17° - 45'
URANUS	♑ 29°- 18'
NEPTUNE	♑ 14°- 19'
PLUTO (R)	♏ 21° - 23'

Chart # 18

SOLAR INGRESS INTO ARIES

4/13/2001 14:30 (EDT) WASHINGTON D.C.

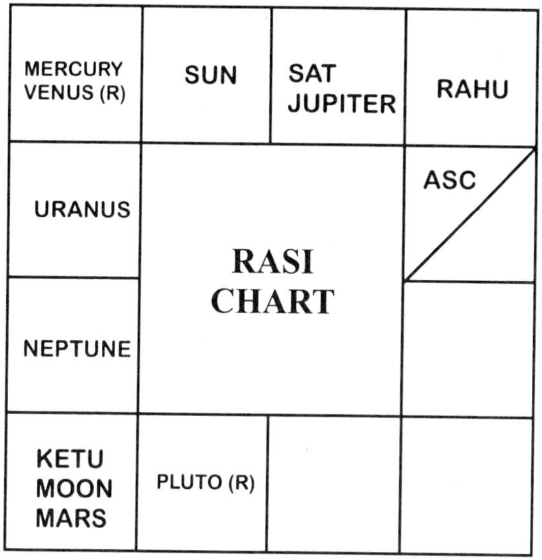

SIDEREAL LONGITUDES	
PLANET	**DEGREES IN SIGN**
ASCENDANT	♋ 28° - 01’
SUN	♈ 0° - 0’
MOON	♐ 9° - 16’
MARS	♐ 0° - 56’
MERCURY	♓ 19° - 49’
JUPITER	♉ 16° - 06’
VENUS (R)	♓ 8° - 25’
SATURN	♉ 5° - 17’
RAHU	♊ 15° - 32’
KETU	♐ 15° - 32’
URANUS	♒ 0° - 07’
NEPTUNE	♑ 14° - 42’
PLUTO (R)	♏ 21° - 12’

Chart # 19

opposition with Ketu and Mars and duly aspected by Uranus. This has serious implications (Please refer to the 12th house at page @@). The 11th house is also badly afflicted due to the placement of Saturn in opposition to Pluto. This indicates some major setback to economy (please see 11th house at page @@@@.

Summing up the above major adverse indications suggests a downturn in the markets in the coming months.

After analyzing the solar ingress charts, lunation charts and eclipse charts it is felt that the following trends are likely, month by month, starting from the month of June, in the stock market for 2001.

June 2001:

Mars will continue to be retrograde for the entire month and beyond until 7/18/2001. Mercury will be retrograde from 6/5/2001 until 6/28/ 2001. Further, Mercury will re-enter Taurus on 6/20/2001 and with thus will conjunct Saturn until 7/7/2001. All these are negative indications. Solar ingress chart for the Sun's entry into Gemini on 6/14/2001 may be seen in Chart # 20. The 7th and the 9th houses are rendered strong which are positive indications. Saturn is adversely placed in the 8th house in opposition with Mars and Pluto, which is a major negative indication.Venus is in trine with Ketu which is also a negative indication. Thus, the chart is predominantly negative.

One total solar eclipse is due to take place on 6/21/2001 (Chart # 21). It will be seen from this chart that the 10th and the 11th houses are rendered very strong which is a positive indication. Mars-Pluto conjunction opposed by Saturn in the 5th house is a negative indication. Uranus's placement in the 8th house is also a negative indication. Mercury, Uranus, Neptune, Mars and Pluto are all retrograde. All these suggest that the market is likely to be volatile in this month also and the 'downs' are likely to predominate over the 'ups' in this month.

SOLAR INGRESS INTO GEMINI

6/14/2001 18:00 (EDT) WASHINGTON D.C.

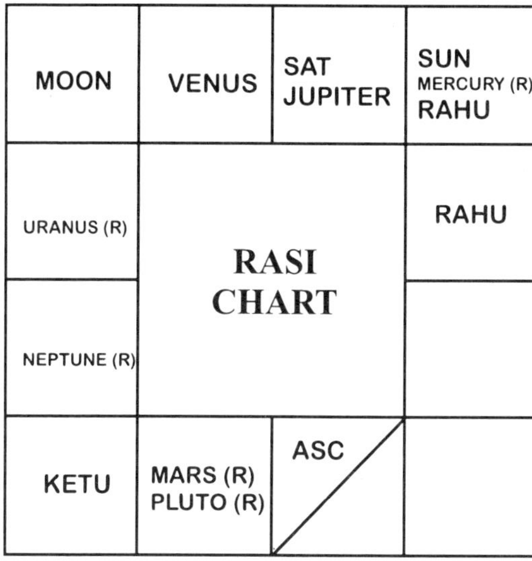

SIDEREAL LONGITUDES	
PLANET	**DEGREES IN SIGN**
ASCENDANT	♎ 29° - 05'
SUN	♊ 0° - 0'
MOON	♓ 8° - 38'
MARS (R)	♏ 28° - 30'
MERCURY (R)	♊ 2° - 30'
JUPITER	♉ 29° - 43'
VENUS	♈ 14° - 23'
SATURN	♉ 13° - 06'
RAHU	♊ 12° - 34'
KETU	♐ 12° - 34'
URANUS (R)	♒ 0° - 51'
NEPTUNE (R)	♑ 14° - 35'
PLUTO (R)	♏ 19° - 46'

Chart # 20

TOTAL SOLAR ECLIPSE ON
6/21/2001 7:57 AM (EDT) WASHINGTON D.C.

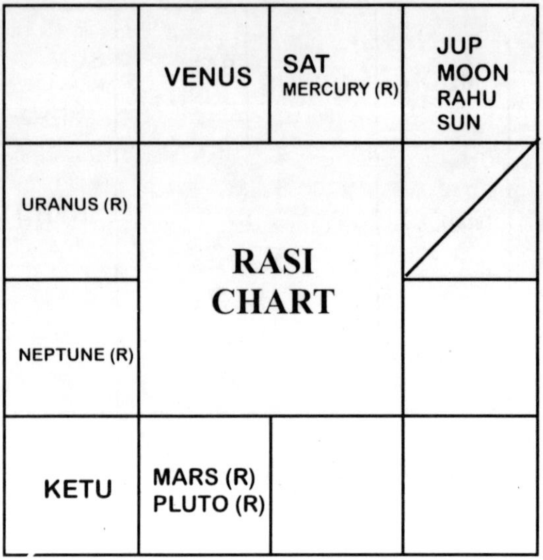

SIDEREAL LONGITUDES	
PLANET	DEGREES IN SIGN
ASCENDANT	♋ 3° - 43'
SUN	♊ 6° - 17'
MOON	♊ 6° - 17'
MARS (R)	♏ 26° - 22'
MERCURY (R)	♉ 29° - 0'
JUPITER	♊ 1° - 14'
VENUS	♈ 21° - 04'
SATURN	♉ 13° - 55'
RAHU	♊ 12° - 28'
KETU	♐ 12° - 28'
URANUS (R)	♒ 0° - 45'
NEPTUNE (R)	♑ 14° - 28'
PLUTO (R)	♏ 19° - 35'

Chart # 21

July 2001:

One partial lunar eclipse is due to occur on 7/5/2001 (Chart # 22). From this chart it may be seen that the 10th and 11th houses are rendered strong due to the placement of Venus, Mercury, Jupiter and Rahu. Saturn's placement in the10th opposed by Mars and Pluto is a major negative indication. Further, Mars, Uranus, Neptune and Pluto are all retrograde. These are all negative indications.

The solar ingress chart for Sun's entry into Cancer on 7/16/2001 is shown in Chart # 23. Here it may be seen that Saturn, Moon and Venus's placement in the 12th opposed by Mars and Pluto is a negative indication. Neptune in the 8th house is also a negative indication. The only positive indication is the placement of Jupiter and Mercury in the Ascendant.

All these suggest that the market is likely to be volatile in this month also and the 'downs' are likely to predominate over the 'ups'.

August 2001:

Mercury will be in Leo from 8/12/2001 and thus will be in trine with Ketu and this situation will last until 8/29/2001. This is a negative indication. Mars will continue to transit very close to Pluto in the sign of Scorpio until 8/26/2001 and will move over to Sagittarius on 8/27/2001. Solar ingress chart for the Sun's entry into Leo on 8/16/2001 may be seen in Chart # 24. Here, the 9th and the 11th houses are rendered strong. These are positive indications. Saturn is adversely placed in the 8th house in opposition to Mars and Pluto. These are major negative indications. Uranus, Neptune, Pluto are in retrogression. Mercury trines with Ketu. These are also negative indications. All these indicate that the market is likely to be volatile for the entire month with predominant downturns.

September 2001:

Saturn will be retrograde from 9/27/2001 onwards until February, 2002. Mars will be in Sagittarius and thus will conjunct

LUNAR ECLIPSE

7/5/2001 11:04 (EDT) WASHINGTON D.C.

<table>
<tr><td></td><td></td><td>VENUS
MERCURY
SAT</td><td>JUPITER
RAHU
SUN</td></tr>
<tr><td>URANUS (R)</td><td colspan="2" rowspan="2">RASI
CHART</td><td></td></tr>
<tr><td>NEPTUNE (R)</td><td>ASC</td></tr>
<tr><td>MOON
KETU</td><td>MARS (R)
PLUTO (R)</td><td></td><td></td></tr>
</table>

SIDEREAL LONGITUDES	
PLANET	**DEGREES IN SIGN**
ASCENDANT	♌ 22° - 07’
SUN	♊ 19° - 46’
MOON	♐ 19° - 46’
MARS (R)	♏ 22° - 39’
MERCURY	♉ 29° - 36’
JUPITER	♊ 4° - 28’
VENUS	♉ 6° - 03’
SATURN	♉ 15° - 36’
RAHU	♊ 12° - 31’
KETU	♐ 12° - 31’
URANUS (R)	♒ 0° - 26’
NEPTUNE (R)	♑ 14° - 09’
PLUTO (R)	♏ 19° - 15’

Chart # 22

SOLAR INGRESS INTO CANCER

7/16/2001 4:30 (EDT) WASHINGTON D.C.

		SAT MOON VENUS	ASC RAHU JUP MERCURY
URANUS (R)	**RASI CHART**		SUN
NEPTUNE (R)			
KETU	MARS (R) PLUTO (R)		

SIDEREAL LONGITUDES	
PLANET	**DEGREES IN SIGN**
ASCENDANT	♊ 10° - 48'
SUN	♋ 0° - 0'
MOON	♉ 0° - 34'
MARS (R)	♏ 21° - 19'
MERCURY	♊ 10° - 32'
JUPITER	♊ 6° - 52'
VENUS	♉ 17° - 50'
SATURN	♉ 16° - 47'
RAHU	♊ 12° - 24'
KETU	♐ 12° - 24'
URANUS (R)	♒ 0° - 07'
NEPTUNE (R)	♑ 13° - 53'
PLUTO (R)	♏ 19° - 02'

Chart # 23

SOLAR INGRESS INTO LEO

8/16/2001 13:00 (EDT) WASHINGTON D.C.

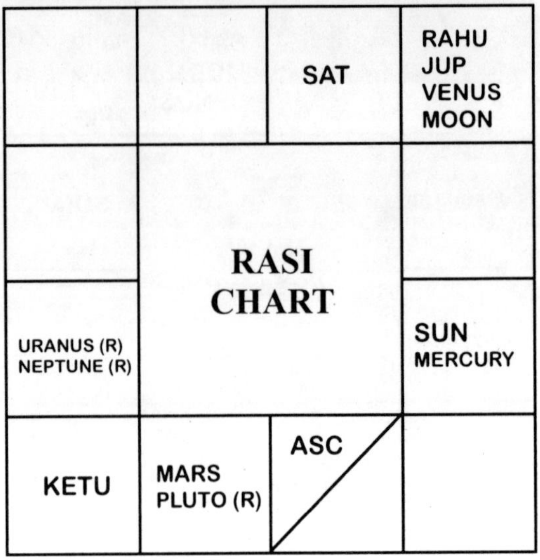

SIDEREAL LONGITUDES	
PLANET	**DEGREES IN SIGN**
ASCENDANT	♎ 18° - 40'
SUN	♌ 0° - 0'
MOON	♊ 25° - 58'
MARS	♏ 26° - 12'
MERCURY	♌ 10° - 46'
JUPITER	♊ 13° - 20'
VENUS	♊ 23° - 45'
SATURN	♉ 19° - 35'
RAHU	♊ 11° - 31'
KETU	♐ 11° - 31'
URANUS (R)	♑ 28° - 56'
NEPTUNE (R)	♑ 13° - 03'
PLUTO (R)	♏ 18° - 40'

Chart # 24

Ketu for the entire month. This is a negative indication. Solar ingress chart for Sun's entry into Virgo on 9/16/2001 may be seen in Chart # 25. Here, the 10th and the 11th houses are rendered strong. These are positive. The 8th house has Rahu in opposition with Mars and Ketu. This is a major negative indication. Venus is in trine with Ketu. Uranus and Neptune both are retrograde. All these mean that the market is likely to be highly volatile with predominant downturns.

October 2001:

Mercury will be retrograde from 10/2/2001 to 10/23/2001. Saturn will be retrograde for the entire month and beyond. These are negative indications. Solar ingress chart for Sun's entry into Libra on 10/17/2001 may be seen in Chart # 26. Here, the 3rd and the 4th houses are rendered strong. These are positive indications. Venus and Mercury are both in trine with Saturn as well as Uranus and Neptune. These are negative indications. Uranus will be retrograde until 10/17/2001 and then will be direct. Neptune will be retrograde for the entire month. These are negative indications. All these mean that the month is likely to be highly volatile with predominant downturns.

November 2001:

Saturn will be retrograde for the entire month. Jupiter will be retrograde from 11/3/2001 and will continue to be so until February 2002 end. Both of these are negative indications. Solar ingress chart for Sun's entry into Scorpio on 11/15/2001 may be seen in Chart # 27. Here, the 3rd and the 11th houses are rendered strong. This a positive indication. Both Venus and Mercury are in trine with Rahu and Jupiter. This is also positive. Saturn is adversely placed in the 10th house in opposition to Pluto. This is a strong negative indication. All these mean that the market is likely to be highly volatile with predominant upturns.

December 2001:

Both Saturn as well as Jupiter will be retrograde for the entire

SOLAR INGRESS INTO VIRGO

9/16/2001 13:00 (EDT) WASHINGTON D.C.

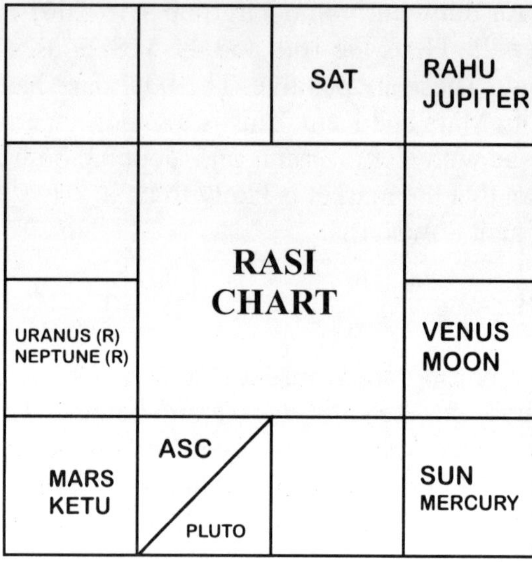

SIDEREAL LONGITUDES	
PLANET	DEGREES IN SIGN
ASCENDANT	♏ 13° - 07'
SUN	♍ 0° - 0'
MOON	♌ 19° - 38'
MARS	♐ 10° - 21'
MERCURY	♍ 26° - 20'
JUPITER	♊ 18° - 26'
VENUS	♌ 0° - 47'
SATURN	♉ 20° - 59'
RAHU	♊ 8° - 50'
KETU	♐ 8° - 50'
URANUS (R)	♑ 27° - 47'
NEPTUNE (R)	♑ 12° - 22'
PLUTO	♏ 18° - 49'

Chart # 25

SOLAR INGRESS INTO LIBRA

10/17/2001 1:00 (EDT) WASHINGTON D.C.

		SAT (R)	RAHU JUPITER
	RASI CHART		ASC
URANUS (R) NEPTUNE (R)			
MARS KETU	PLUTO	SUN MOON	VENUS MERCURY (R)

SIDEREAL LONGITUDES	
PLANET	DEGREES IN SIGN
ASCENDANT	♋ 13° - 08'
SUN	♎ 0° - 0'
MOON	♎ 5° - 29'
MARS	♐ 29° - 02'
MERCURY (R)	♍ 23 - 22'
JUPITER	♊ 21° - 22'
VENUS	♍ 8° - 15'
SATURN (R)	♉ 20° - 43'
RAHU	♊ 5° - 29'
KETU	♐ 5° - 29'
URANUS (R)	♑ 27° - 06'
NEPTUNE (R)	♑ 12° - 07'
PLUTO	♏ 19° - 07'

Chart # 26

SOLAR INGRESS INTO SCORPIO

11/15/2001 23:35 (EST) WASHINGTON D.C.

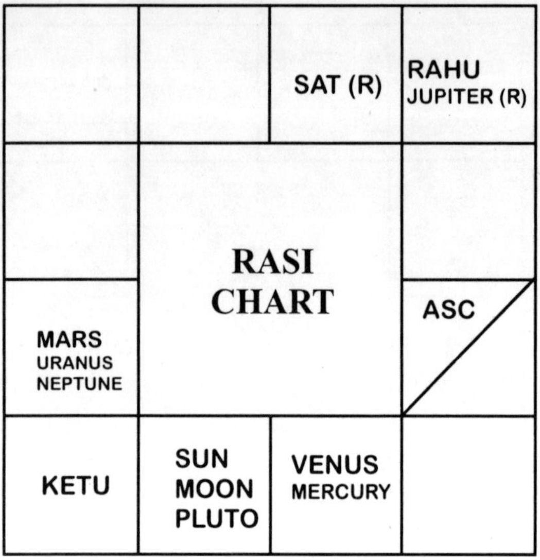

SIDEREAL LONGITUDES	
PLANET	**DEGREES IN SIGN**
ASCENDANT	♌ 1° - 38'
SUN	♏ 0° - 0'
MOON	♏ 11° - 40'
MARS	♑ 19° - 43'
MERCURY	♎ 19 - 17'
JUPITER (R)	♊ 21° - 30'
VENUS	♎ 15° - 40'
SATURN (R)	♉ 18° - 59'
RAHU	♊ 3° - 33'
KETU	♐ 3° - 33'
URANUS	♑ 27° - 08'
NEPTUNE	♑ 12° - 21'
PLUTO	♏ 20° - 25'

Chart # 27

month and beyond. Mercury will conjunct Ketu from 12/12/2001 to 12/30/2001. These are negative indications. One annular solar eclipse will occur on 12/14/2001 (Chart #28). Here, Mars is adversely placed in the 10th house aspected by Rahu and Saturn. This is a major negative indication. Mercury, and Ketu's placement in the 8th house is a negative indication. Saturn and Jupiter are retrograde. These are all negative. Jupiter in the 2nd is the only positive indication.
Solar ingress chart for Sun's entry into Sagittarius on 12/15/2001 may be seen in Chart # 29. Here, the 8th house is badly afflicted due to the presence Moon, Rahu and Jupiter in opposition with Ketu. Saturn is adversely placed in the 7th house in opposition with Pluto is aspected by Mars. These are all major negative indications. The only positive is Venus and Mercury in the 2nd house.

One penumbral lunar eclipse will occur on 12/30/2001 (Chart # 30). This eclipse chart is almost identical to the above mentioned Solar Ingress chart (Chart # 29). In all the three charts described above major negative indications are present. This indicates some major adverse development in this month which is likely to impact the market with strong bearish trends.

Market Projections for the year 2002:

There are five eclipses (two Solar and three Lunar eclipses) due in this year.

1) Penumbral eclipse of the Moon due on May 26, 2002.
2) Annular solar eclipse due on June 10, 2002.
3) Penumbral Lunar eclipse due on June 24, 2002.
4) Penumbral lunar eclipse due on Nov 19, 2002.
5) Total solar eclipse due on December 3, 2002.

Transits of importance in the Year 2002:

1) Jupiter will transit the Gemini from June 16 onwards and will remain there for the rest of this year and beyond until July 6, 2003.

SOLAR ECLIPSE

12/14/2001 15:48 (EST) WASHINGTON D.C.

		ASC / SAT (R)	RAHU JUPITER (R)
MARS	RASI CHART		
URANUS NEPTUNE			
MERCURY KETU	SUN MOON VENUS PLUTO		

SIDEREAL LONGITUDES	
PLANET	**DEGREES IN SIGN**
ASCENDANT	♉ 15° - 12'
SUN	♏ 29° - 03'
MOON	♏ 29° - 03'
MARS	♒ 10° - 27'
MERCURY	♐ 4° - 35'
JUPITER (R)	♊ 19° - 01'
VENUS	♏ 21° - 43'
SATURN (R)	♉ 16° - 41'
RAHU	♊ 3° - 15'
KETU	♐ 3° - 15'
URANUS	♑ 27° - 52'
NEPTUNE	♑ 13° - 01'
PLUTO	♏ 21° - 31'

Chart # 28

SOLAR INGRESS INTO SAGITTARIUS

12/15/2001 14:30 (EST) WASHINGTON D.C.

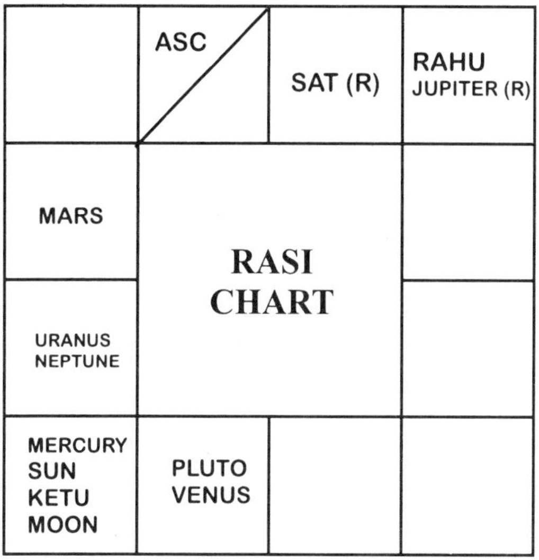

SIDEREAL LONGITUDES	
PLANET	**DEGREES IN SIGN**
ASCENDANT	♈ 22° - 39'
SUN	♐ 0° - 0'
MOON	♐ 11° - 20'
MARS	♒ 11° - 09'
MERCURY	♐ 6° - 05'
JUPITER (R)	♊ 18° - 54'
VENUS	♏ 22° - 54'
SATURN (R)	♉ 16° - 36'
RAHU	♊ 3° - 15'
KETU	♐ 3° - 15'
URANUS	♑ 27° - 54'
NEPTUNE	♑ 13° - 02'
PLUTO	♏ 21° - 33'

Chart # 29

2) Rahu will transit Taurus and Ketu will transit Scorpio from March 2 this year and will remain there for the rest of the year and beyond until August 29, 2003.

On May 13, 2002, seven planets will congregate in the sign of Taurus. Prior to this, Mars and Saturn will be conjunct on May 5 on the same longitude and this conjunction occurs in Rohini nakshatra. This is likely to have an impact on the financial markets in the months following this conjunction.

Uranus moves into Aquarius in January 29, 2002 and will remain the same sign for the entire year. However, Uranus will become retrograde from June 3rd until November 4th. Neptune will transit Capricorn for the entire year. Neptune will become retrograde from May 14th and will remain so until October 19th then becomes direct. Pluto will transit Scorpio for the whole year. Pluto will become retrograde from March 21st and will become direct form August 26th.

General Observations for the Year 2002:

Lunation in the Sign of Pisces on 4/12/2002:

Please see Chart# 34. This chart has one major negative indication due to adverse placement of Mars, Saturn and Rahu in the 10th house in opposition with Ketu and Pluto. This suggests some serious implications (please refer to the 10th house on Page 78).

Solar Ingress into Aries on 4/13/2002:

Please Chart # 35. This chart has major neegative indications due to the adverse placement of Mars, Saturn and Rahu in the 8th house in opposition with Ketu and Pluto. These also suggest serious implications. Please refer to the Eighth House on Page 77.

After analyzing the solar ingress charts, lunation charts and the eclipse charts it is felt that the following trends are likely, month by month, for the year 2002.

January 2002:

As we commence the New Year 2002, the lingering bearish effects of December 2001 eclipse will continue into January 2002. Further, both Jupiter and Saturn will be retrograde for the whole month. Mercury will be retrograde from 1/19/2002 and will remain so for the rest of the month and beyond and will be in trine to Saturn. The solar ingress chart for Sun's entry into Capricorn on 1/14/2002 may be seen in Chart # 31. In this chart Venus is in trine with Ketu. Saturn is adversely placed in the 8th house opposed by Pluto. Mercury is in trine with Saturn. All these are negative. The only positive is Jupiter in the 9th. These indicate that the market is likely to be bearish for the entire month of January.

February 2002:

Jupiter will be retrograde for the whole month. Saturn will be retrograde until 2/7/2002. Mercury will be retrograde until 2/7/2002 and will also be trine to Saturn. Solar ingress chart for Sun's entry into Aquarius on 2/12/2002 may be seen in Chart # 32. In this chart, the 9th house is rendered strong. Jupiter in the ascendant is positive. Venus trines Rahu and Jupiter is also positive. Mars in the 10th house is a strong negative indication. Mercury and Neptune in the 8th house is another negative indication. All these mean that in the first fortnight the market is likely to be bearish and in the second fortnight the market is likely to be highly volatile.

March 2002:

Mercury will trine Rahu for the most part of this month. The solar ingress chart for the Sun's entry into Pisces on 3/14/2002 may be seen in Chart # 33. Here, the 1st, 9th, 10th and the 11th houses are rendered strong. These are all positive indications. Saturn and Rahu in the 12th in opposition with Ketu and Pluto is a major negative. Neptune's placement in the 8th house is another negative indication. All these indicate that the market is likely to be volatile with predominant downturns.

LUNAR ECLIPSE

12/30/2001 5:42 (EST) WASHINGTON D.C.

<table>
<tr><td></td><td></td><td>SAT (R)</td><td>MOON
RAHU
JUPITER (R)</td></tr>
<tr><td>MARS</td><td colspan="2" rowspan="2">RASI
CHART</td><td></td></tr>
<tr><td>URANUS
NEPTUNE</td><td></td></tr>
<tr><td>MERCURY
KETU
SUN
VENUS</td><td>ASC
PLUTO</td><td></td><td></td></tr>
</table>

SIDEREAL LONGITUDES	
PLANET	DEGREES IN SIGN
ASCENDANT	♏ 20^{0} - 20'
SUN	♐ 14^{0} - 55'
MOON	♐ 14^{0} - 55'
MARS	♒ 21^{0} - 51'
MERCURY	♐ 29^{0} - 17'
JUPITER (R)	♊ 16^{0} - 59'
VENUS	♐ 11^{0} - 19'
SATURN (R)	♉ 15^{0} - 32'
RAHU	♊ 3^{0} - 19'
KETU	♐ 3^{0} - 19'
URANUS	♑ 28^{0} - 30'
NEPTUNE	♑ 13^{0} - 30'
PLUTO	♏ 22^{0} - 05'

Chart # 30

SOLAR INGRESS INTO CAPRICORN

1/14/2002 1:00 (EST) WASHINGTON D.C.

MARS		SAT (R)	RAHU JUPITER (R)
	RASI CHART		
MERCURY MOON SUN URANUS NEPTUNE			
VENUS KETU	PLUTO	ASC	

SIDEREAL LONGITUDES	
PLANET	DEGREES IN SIGN
ASCENDANT	♎ 5° - 27'
SUN	♑ 0° - 0'
MOON	♑ 7° - 49'
MARS	♓ 2° - 41'
MERCURY	♑ 18° - 44'
JUPITER (R)	♊ 15° - 01'
VENUS	♐ 29° - 57'
SATURN (R)	♉ 14° - 43'
RAHU	♊ 3° - 09'
KETU	♐ 3° - 09'
URANUS	♑ 29° - 13'
NEPTUNE	♑ 14° - 02'
PLUTO	♏ 22° - 36'

Chart # 31

SOLAR INGRESS INTO AQUARIIUS

2/12/2002 14:00 (EST) WASHINGTON D.C.

<table>
<tr><td>MARS</td><td></td><td>SAT</td><td>ASC
RAHU
JUPITER (R)</td></tr>
<tr><td>SUN
VENUS
MOON
URANUS</td><td colspan="2" rowspan="2">RASI
CHART</td><td></td></tr>
<tr><td>NEPTUNE
MERCURY</td><td></td></tr>
<tr><td>KETU</td><td>PLUTO</td><td></td><td></td></tr>
</table>

SIDEREAL LONGITUDES	
PLANET	**DEGREES IN SIGN**
ASCENDANT	♊ 15° - 58'
SUN	♒ 0° - 0'
MOON	♒ 5° - 10'
MARS	♓ 24° - 05'
MERCURY	♑ 5° - 40'
JUPITER (R)	♊ 12° - 12'
VENUS	♒ 7° - 02'
SATURN	♉ 14° - 10'
RAHU	♊ 1° - 36'
KETU	♐ 1° - 36'
URANUS	♒ 0° - 52'
NEPTUNE	♑ 15° - 09'
PLUTO	♏ 23° - 23'

Chart # 32

SOLAR INGRESS INTO PISCES

3/14/2002 11:00 (EST) WASHINGTON D.C.

<table>
<tr><td>VENUS
MOON
SUN</td><td>MARS</td><td>RAHU
SAT</td><td>ASC
JUPITER</td></tr>
<tr><td>MERCURY
URANUS</td><td colspan="2" rowspan="2">RASI
CHART</td><td></td></tr>
<tr><td>NEPTUNE</td><td></td></tr>
<tr><td></td><td>KETU
PLUTO</td><td></td><td></td></tr>
</table>

SIDEREAL LONGITUDES	
PLANET	DEGREES IN SIGN
ASCENDANT	♊ 1° - 58’
SUN	♓ 0° - 0’
MOON	♓ 6° - 19’
MARS	♈ 15° - 18’
MERCURY	♒ 10° - 16’
JUPITER	♊ 12° - 01’
VENUS	♓ 14° - 19’
SATURN	♉ 15° - 14’
RAHU	♉ 28° - 22’
KETU	♏ 28° - 22’
URANUS	♒ 2° - 33’
NEPTUNE	♑ 16° - 09’
PLUTO	♏ 23° - 44’

Chart # 33

April 2002:

The lunation chart for the lunation in Pisces on 4/12/2002 may be seen in Chart # 34. In this chart, the 9th and 11th houses are rendered very strong. Mars, Saturn and Rahu in the 10th, opposed by Ketu and Pluto is a major negative indication. Furthermore, Saturn is placed in Rohini nakshatra which is believed to be a major negative point in Vedic Astrology. Lunation occurs in the 8th house which is also a major negative indication. These negative indications suggest some major international developments that can impact the market with high volatility with predominant downturns during this month.

The solar ingress chart for Sun's entry into Aries on 4/13/2002 may be seen in Chart # 35. Here, Mars, Saturn and Rahu very adversely placed in the 8th house in opposition with Ketu and Pluto. Further, Saturn will transit through Rohini Nakshatra, which is another major negative indication. Mars will also transit Rohini Nakshatra from April 20th onwards. These suggest some major adverse developments of worldwide impact. Jupiter in the 9th is the only positive point. All these indicate that the market is likely to be highly volatile in this month with predominant downturns.

May 2002:

Mars, Mercury and Saturn will continue to be in Taurus. Further, Mercury will be retrograde from 5/16/2002 and continue to be so for the rest of the month and beyond until 6/8/2002. Solar ingress chart for the Sun's entry into Taurus on 5/14/2002 may be seen in Chart # 36.

Unique feature in this chart is the congregation of 7 planets in Taurus in opposition by Pluto and Ketu. Further, Saturn will continue to transit Rohini nakshatra. Mars will also continue to transit Rohini nakshatra until the 10th of this month. These are all major negative indications suggesting some major worldwide developments affecting the markets.

LUNATION IN PISCES

4/12/2002 15:20 (EDT) WASHINGTON D.C.

MOON SUN	MERCURY VENUS	MARS SAT RAHU	JUPITER
URANUS	**RASI CHART**		
NEPTUNE			ASC
	KETU PLUTO (R)		

SIDEREAL LONGITUDES	
PLANET	**DEGREES IN SIGN**
ASCENDANT	♌ 7° - 0'
SUN	♓ 28° - 48'
MOON	♓ 28° - 38'
MARS	♉ 5° - 28'
MERCURY	♈ 4° - 49'
JUPITER	♊ 14° - 28'
VENUS	♈ 20° - 17'
SATURN	♉ 17° - 38'
RAHU	♉ 25° - 26'
KETU	♏ 25° - 26'
URANUS	♒ 3° - 54'
NEPTUNE	♑ 16° - 50'
PLUTO (R)	♏ 23° - 35'

Chart # 34

SOLAR INGRESS INTO ARIES

4/13/2002 20:30 (EDT) WASHINGTON D.C.

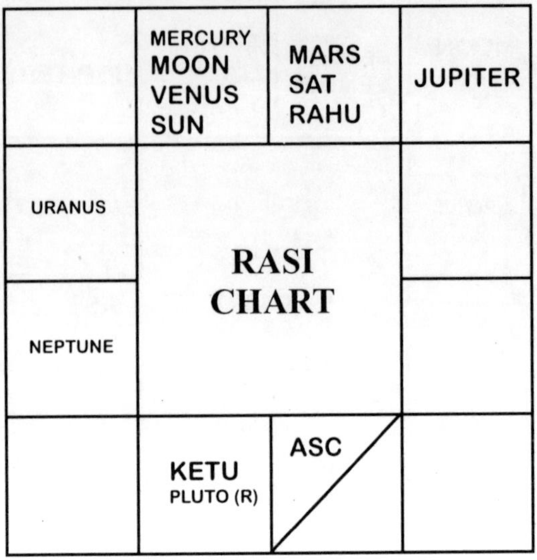

SIDEREAL LONGITUDES	
PLANET	**DEGREES IN SIGN**
ASCENDANT	♎ 10° - 12'
SUN	♈ 0° - 0'
MOON	♈ 13° - 27'
MARS	♉ 6° - 18'
MERCURY	♈ 7° - 21'
JUPITER	♊ 14° - 37'
VENUS	♈ 21 - 47'
SATURN	♉ 17° - 45'
RAHU	♉ 25° - 15'
KETU	♏ 25° - 15'
URANUS	♒ 3° - 57'
NEPTUNE	♑ 16° - 51'
PLUTO (R)	♏ 23° - 34'

Chart # 35

SOLAR INGRESS INTO TAURUS

5/14/2002 17:30 (EDT) WASHINGTON D.C.

		SAT, MARS VENUS, SUN MOON, RAHU MERCURY	JUPITER
URANUS	RASI CHART		
NEPTUNE (R)			
	KETU PLUTO (R)		ASC

SIDEREAL LONGITUDES	
PLANET	**DEGREES IN SIGN**
ASCENDANT	♍ 28° - 35'
SUN	♉ 0° - 0'
MOON	♉ 28° - 32'
MARS	♉ 27° - 06'
MERCURY	♉ 16° - 04'
JUPITER	♊ 19° - 24'
VENUS	♉ 29° - 18'
SATURN	♉ 21° - 17'
RAHU	♉ 24° - 0'
KETU	♏ 24° - 0'
URANUS	♒ 4° - 47'
NEPTUNE (R)	♑ 17° - 05'
PLUTO (R)	♏ 22° - 59'

Chart # 36

A penumbral lunar eclipse will take place on 5/26/2002 (Chart # 37). Here, the only positive indication is concerning the first house which is rendered strong. The 12th house has Saturn, Sun and Rahu in opposition with Pluto and Ketu which is major negative indication. Neptune's placement in the 8th is also a negative indication. All these indicate that the market is likely to be highly volatile with a predominant downturn occurring in the first fortnight.

June 2002: Mercury will be conjunct Rahu for the entire month. Mercury will be retrograde until 6/8/2002 and becomes direct for the entire month in Gemini. Mercury's conjunction with Rahu is a major positive indication. An annular solar eclipse will take place on 6/10/2002. See Chart # 38.

Here, the 1st, 7th and the 8th houses are badly afflicted. The 9th house has Venus placed therein which is positive. Solar ingress chart for 6/14/2002 may be seen in Chart# 39. Here, the 1st, 5th, 6th and the 11th houses are badly afflicted. Thus the negative indications are predominant.
One penumbral lunar eclipse will take place on 6/24/2002 (Chart # 40). Here, Mars and Sun are adversely placed in the 8th house. In addition, the 1st, 3rd and 7th houses are badly afflicted. Venus in the 9th house is a positive indication. All this indicates that market is likely to be highly volatile for the entire month.

July 2002:

For the last ten days of this month Mercury will be in trine with Ketu, which is a negative indication. Jupiter will transit Cancer from 7/6/2002 and will conjunct Mars, which is a positive indication. Solar ingress chart for the Sun's entry into Cancer 7/16/2002 may be seen in Chart # 41.

Here, Saturn and Rahus' placement in the 10th, in opposition to Pluto and Ketu is a major negative indication. Venus in the Ascendant and Mercury in the 11th are very positive. All this indicates that the market is likely to be volatile with predominant downturns.

LUNAR ECLIPSE (PENUMBRAL)

5/26/2002 7:52 (EDT) WASHINGTON D.C.

		MERCURY(R) SAT SUN RAHU	ASC VENUS MARS JUPITER
URANUS	RASI CHART		
NEPTUNE (R)			
	KETU MOON PLUTO (R)		

SIDEREAL LONGITUDES	
PLANET	DEGREES IN SIGN
ASCENDANT	♊ 10° - 55'
SUN	♉ 11° - 10'
MOON	♏ 11° - 10'
MARS	♊ 4° - 47'
MERCURY (R)	♉ 12° - 23'
JUPITER	♊ 21° - 35'
VENUS	♊ 13° - 12'
SATURN	♉ 22° - 45'
RAHU	♉ 23° - 56'
KETU	♏ 23° - 56'
URANUS	♒ 4° - 55'
NEPTUNE (R)	♑ 17° - 03'
PLUTO (R)	♏ 22° - 41'

Chart # 37

SOLAR ECLIPSE (ANNULAR)

6/10/2002 19:48 (EDT) WASHINGTON D.C.

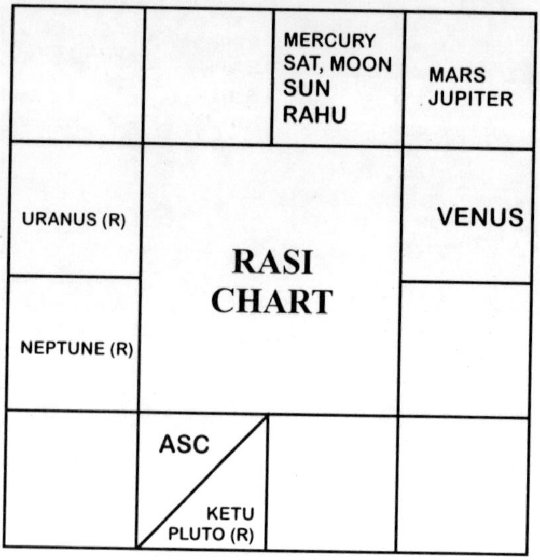

SIDEREAL LONGITUDES	
PLANET	**DEGREES IN SIGN**
ASCENDANT	♏ 17° - 35'
SUN	♉ 26° - 01'
MOON	♉ 26° - 01'
MARS	♊ 14° - 58'
MERCURY	♉ 7° - 40'
JUPITER	♊ 24° - 44'
VENUS	♋ 1° - 35'
SATURN	♉ 24° - 45'
RAHU	♉ 23° - 58'
KETU	♏ 23° - 58'
URANUS (R)	♒ 4° - 55'
NEPTUNE (R)	♑ 16° - 53'
PLUTO (R)	♏ 22° - 17'

Chart # 38

SOLAR INGRESS INTO GEMINI

6/14/2002 23:50 (EDT) WASHINGTON D.C.

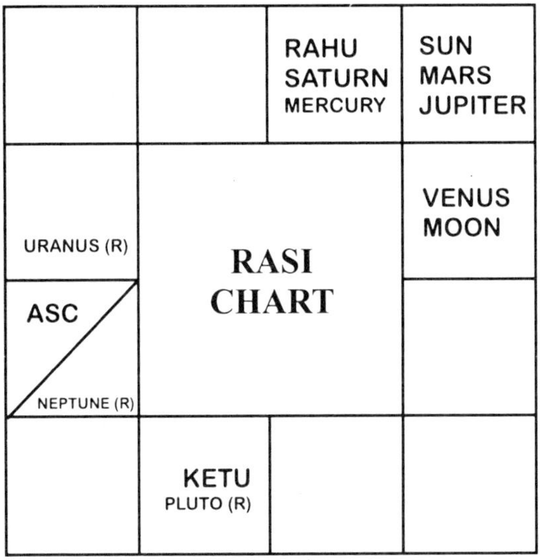

SIDEREAL LONGITUDES	
PLANET	**DEGREES IN SIGN**
ASCENDANT	♑ 24° - 42'
SUN	♊ 0° - 0'
MOON	♋ 22° - 21'
MARS	♊ 17° - 41'
MERCURY	♉ 9° - 03'
JUPITER	♊ 25° - 37'
VENUS	♋ 6° - 28'
SATURN	♉ 25° - 18'
RAHU	♉ 23° - 57'
KETU	♏ 23° - 57'
URANUS (R)	♒ 4° - 53'
NEPTUNE (R)	♑ 16° - 49'
PLUTO (R)	♏ 22° - 10'

Chart # 39

LUNAR ECLIPSE (PENUMBRAL)

6/24/2002 17:43 (EDT) WASHINGTON D.C.

		RAHU SATURN MERCURY	SUN MARS JUPITER
URANUS (R)	RASI CHART		VENUS
NEPTUNE (R)			
MOON	ASC / KETU PLUTO (R)		

SIDEREAL LONGITUDES	
PLANET	**DEGREES IN SIGN**
ASCENDANT	♏ 3° - 20'
SUN	♊ 9° - 18'
MOON	♐ 9° - 18'
MARS	♊ 24° - 01'
MERCURY	♉ 17° - 06'
JUPITER	♊ 27° - 43'
VENUS	♋ 17° - 50'
SATURN	♉ 26° - 33'
RAHU	♉ 23° - 58'
KETU	♏ 23° - 58'
URANUS (R)	♒ 4° - 45'
NEPTUNE (R)	♑ 16° - 38'
PLUTO (R)	♏ 21° - 55'

Chart# 40

SOLAR INGRESS INTO CANCER

7/16/2002 10:45 (EDT) WASHINGTON D.C.

		SAT RAHU	MERCURY
URANUS (R)	**RASI CHART**		SUN MARS JUPITER
NEPTUNE (R)			ASC / VENUS
	KETU PLUTO (R)		MOON

SIDEREAL LONGITUDES	
PLANET	**DEGREES IN SIGN**
ASCENDANT	♌ 26° - 49'
SUN	♋ 0° - 0'
MOON	♍ 22° - 15'
MARS	♋ 8° - 01'
MERCURY	♊ 24° - 43'
JUPITER	♋ 2° - 31'
VENUS	♌ 12° - 32'
SATURN	♉ 29° - 14'
RAHU	♉ 23° - 24'
KETU	♏ 23° - 24'
URANUS (R)	♒ 4° - 13'
NEPTUNE (R)	♑ 16° - 08'
PLUTO (R)	♏ 21° - 25'

Chart # 41

August 2002:

Mars will have sign conjunction with Jupiter until 8/21/2002, which is a positive indication. Solar ingress chart for Sun's entry into Leo on 8/16/2002 may be seen in Chart # 42.

Here, the 7th and the 9th houses are rendered very strong. There is a Vipareeta Raja Yoga formed due to the conjunction of the lords of the 6th and the 8th. These are positive indications.

The 1st, 5th, 6th and 11th are badly afflicted. Thus, the positive and negative indications seem to be balanced. All this indicates the market is likely to become bullish.

September 2002:

Ketu and Pluto will continue to be very close to each other in the Scorpio sign for the entire month. This is a negative indication. Solar ingress chart for Sun's entry into Virgo on 9/16/2002 may be seen in Chart # 43.

Ketu-Pluto conjunction falls in the 10th house opposed by Rahu and aspected by Mars. This is a major negative indication. 1st, 5th and the 8th houses are also afflicted. All this are negative. The only positive is the good placement of Venus in the 9th house. Mercury will become retrograde from 9/15/2002. All these indicate that the market is likely to become bearish due to some major adverse development.

October 2002:

Mercury will be retrograde until 10/05/2002 and then becomes direct. Venus will become retrograde from 10/11/2002 and will remain so for the remaining portion of this month and beyond until 11/21/2002. Saturn will become retrograde from 10/11/2002 and will remain so for the remaining portion of this month and beyond until February, 2003. Solar ingress chart for Sun's entry into Libra on 10/17/2002 may be seen in Chart # 44.

SOLAR INGRESS INTO LEO

8/16/2002 19:00 (EDT) WASHINGTON D.C.

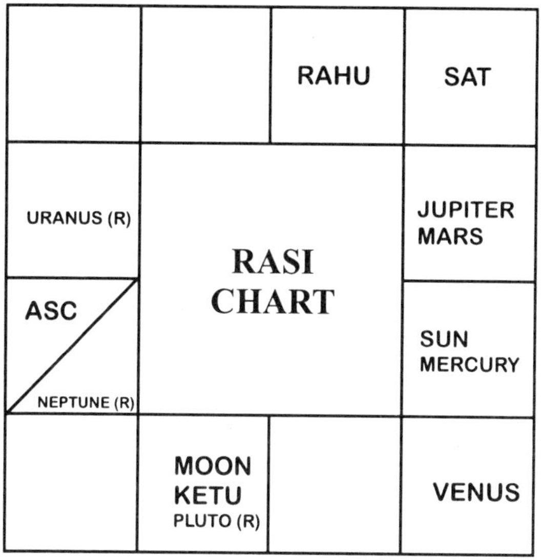

SIDEREAL LONGITUDES	
PLANET	**DEGREES IN SIGN**
ASCENDANT	♑ 10° - 39'
SUN	♌ 0° - 0'
MOON	♏ 19° - 24'
MARS	♋ 28° - 03'
MERCURY	♌ 22° - 58'
JUPITER	♋ 9° - 26'
VENUS	♍ 15° - 53'
SATURN	♊ 2° - 32'
RAHU	♉ 21° - 36'
KETU	♏ 21° - 36'
URANUS (R)	♒ 3° - 05'
NEPTUNE (R)	♑ 15° - 17'
PLUTO (R)	♏ 21° - 01'

Chart # 42

SOLAR INGRESS INTO VIRGO

9/16/2002 19:00 (EDT) WASHINGTON D.C.

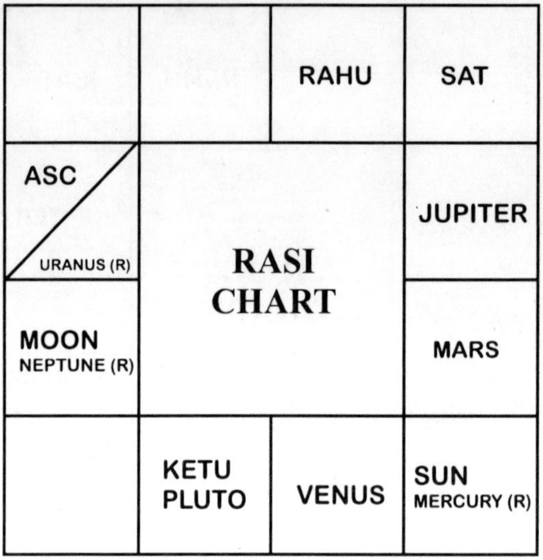

SIDEREAL LONGITUDES	
PLANET	DEGREES IN SIGN
ASCENDANT	♒ 25° - 34’
SUN	♍ 0° - 0’
MOON	♑ 8° - 14’
MARS	♌ 17° - 47’
MERCURY (R)	♍ 19° - 06’
JUPITER	♋ 15° - 44’
VENUS	♎ 12° - 39’
SATURN	♊ 4° - 38’
RAHU	♉ 18° - 36’
KETU	♏ 18° - 36’
URANUS (R)	♒ 1° - 54’
NEPTUNE (R)	♑ 14° - 36’
PLUTO	♏ 21° - 08’

Chart # 43

SOLAR INGRESS INTO LIBRA

10/17/2002 7:00 (EDT) WASHINGTON D.C.

		RAHU	SAT (R)
MOON URANUS (R)	RASI CHART		JUPITER
NEPTUNE (R)			
	KETU	SUN VENUS (R)	ASC / MARS MERCURY

SIDEREAL LONGITUDES	
PLANET	DEGREES IN SIGN
ASCENDANT	♍ 25° - 14'
SUN	♎ 0° - 0'
MOON	♒ 18° - 06'
MARS	♍ 7° - 12'
MERCURY	♍ 12° - 54'
JUPITER	♋ 20° - 43'
VENUS (R)	♎ 20° - 49'
SATURN (R)	♊ 5° - 09'
RAHU	♉ 15° - 53'
KETU	♏ 15° - 53'
URANUS (R)	♒ 1° - 08'
NEPTUNE (R)	♑ 14° - 18'
PLUTO	♏ 21° - 43'

Chart # 44

Here, the 11th house is rendered very strong. Mercury trines Rahu as well as Neptune. Venus is strongly placed in the 2nd house. Saturn's placement in the 10th house is a major negative indication. All these indicate that the market is likely to be volatile with predominant upturns.

November 2002:

Venus will be retrograde until 11/20/2002 and then becomes direct. Saturn will be retrograde for the entire month and beyond until February, 2003. Mercury will enter Scorpio on 11/16/2002 and will conjunct Ketu. This is a negative indication. The Solar ingress chart for Sun's entry into Scorpio on 11/16/2002 may be seen in Chart # 45.

Here, the 1st, 9th and the 10th houses are rendered very strong. The 2nd, 8th and the 12th houses are very badly afflicted. Thus, the chart has both positive and negative indications.

One penumbral lunar eclipse will take place on 11/19/2002 (Chart # 46). The 2nd and the 5th houses are rendered very strong. The 1st, 4th, 6th, 8th and the 12th are afflicted. All these indicate that the market is likely to be volatile in the first half and is likely to be bearish in the second half of this month.

December 2002:

Venus and Mars will have sign conjunction in Libra for the entire month. A total Solar eclipse will occur on 12/4/2002 (Chart # 47). Here, the 2nd and the 11th houses are rendered strong. The 3rd house is severely afflicted and Saturn is adversely placed in the 10th house in the eclipse chart. These are major negative indications.

From 12/5/2002 Jupiter will become retrograde and remain so until April, 2003. The solar ingress chart for Sun's entry into Sagittarius on 12/15/2002 may be seen in Chart # 48.

Here, the 1st, 4th and the 10th houses are rendered very strong.

The 5th, 8th and the 12th are afflicted. Thus, the chart has both positive and negative indications.

Some scandal or similar development is likely to impact the market which is likely to be volatile with predominant downturns. Please see Third House on Page @@@.

OM----TAT----SAT.

SOLAR INGRESS INTO SCORPIO

11/16/2002 6:45 (EDT) WASHINGTON D.C.

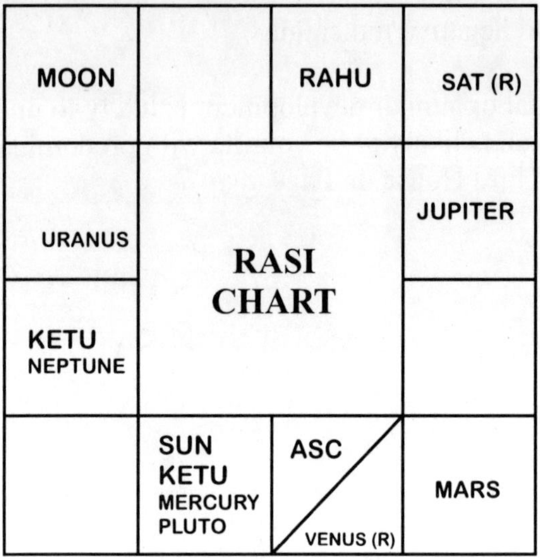

SIDEREAL LONGITUDES	
PLANET	**DEGREES IN SIGN**
ASCENDANT	♎ 15° - 49'
SUN	♏ 0° - 0'
MOON	♓ 20° - 28'
MARS	♍ 26° - 22'
MERCURY	♏ 1° - 19'
JUPITER	♋ 23° - 41'
VENUS (R)	♎ 6° - 38'
SATURN (R)	♊ 4° - 03'
RAHU	♉ 14° - 51'
KETU	♏ 14° - 51'
URANUS	♒ 1° - 04'
NEPTUNE	♑ 14° - 30'
PLUTO	♏ 22° - 40'

Chart # 45

LUNAR ECLIPSE (PENUMBRAL)

11/19/2002 20:34 (EST) WASHINGTON D.C.

<table>
<tr><td></td><td></td><td>RAHU
MOON</td><td>ASC
SAT (R)</td></tr>
<tr><td>URANUS</td><td colspan="2" rowspan="2">RASI
CHART</td><td>JUPITER</td></tr>
<tr><td>NEPTUNE</td><td></td></tr>
<tr><td></td><td>SUN
KETU
MERCURY
PLUTO</td><td>VENUS (R)</td><td>MARS</td></tr>
</table>

SIDEREAL LONGITUDES	
PLANET	**DEGREES IN SIGN**
ASCENDANT	♊ 28° - 20'
SUN	♏ 3° - 39'
MOON	♉ 3° - 39'
MARS	♍ 28° - 42'
MERCURY	♏ 7° - 01'
JUPITER	♋ 23° - 52'
VENUS (R)	♎ 6° - 11'
SATURN (R)	♊ 3° - 49'
RAHU	♉ 14° - 45'
KETU	♏ 14° - 45'
URANUS	♒ 1° - 07'
NEPTUNE	♑ 14° - 34'
PLUTO	♏ 22° - 48'

Chart # 46

TOTAL SOLAR ECLIPSE

12/4/2002 2:34 (EST) WASHINGTON D.C.

		RAHU	SAT (R)
URANUS	RASI CHART		JUPITER
NEPTUNE			
	SUN KETU MOON MERCURY PLUTO	VENUS MARS	ASC

SIDEREAL LONGITUDES	
PLANET	DEGREES IN SIGN
ASCENDANT	♍ 21° - 45'
SUN	♏ 18° - 04'
MOON	♏ 18° - 04'
MARS	♎ 7° - 51'
MERCURY	♏ 29° - 09'
JUPITER	♋ 24° - 12'
VENUS	♎ 9° - 18'
SATURN (R)	♊ 2° - 47'
RAHU	♉ 14° - 48'
KETU	♏ 14° - 48'
URANUS	♒ 1° - 23'
NEPTUNE	♑ 14° - 51'
PLUTO	♏ 23° - 20'

Chart # 47

SOLAR INGRESS INTO SAGITTARIUS

12/15/2002 20:30 (EST) WASHINGTON D.C.

	MOON	RAHU	SAT (R)
URANUS	RASI CHART		ASC / JUP (R)
NEPTUNE			
MERCURY SUN	KETU PLUTO	VENUS MARS	

SIDEREAL LONGITUDES	
PLANET	DEGREES IN SIGN
ASCENDANT	♋ 18° - 05'
SUN	♐ 0° - 0'
MOON	♈ 17° - 53'
MARS	♎ 15° - 24'
MERCURY	♐ 16° - 55'
JUPITER (R)	♋ 23° - 59'
VENUS	♎ 16° - 21'
SATURN (R)	♊ 1° - 50'
RAHU	♉ 14° - 48'
KETU	♏ 14° - 48'
URANUS	♒ 1° - 44'
NEPTUNE	♑ 15° - 10'
PLUTO	♏ 23° - 47'

Chart # 48

Bibliography

1. Dr. B.V. Raman. Astrology for beginners (1940).

2. Dr. B.V. Raman. How to Judge a Horoscope (1941).

3. LCdr.David Williams (Retd.). Financial Astrology (1982).

4. Joan McEvers. Financial Astrology for the 1990s (1989).

5. Pandit Hardev Trivedi. "Vyapar Ratna" (Hindi language).

6. Pandit Ganga Prasad Jyotishacharya, "Vyapar Chintamani" (Hindi language), (1957).

7. Martha Betz & Keith Betz. The Betz Ephemeris 1940-2040. (2001).

8. T.G. Butaney. Forecasting prices with forecast of shares etc. (1940).

9. R.G. Krishnan. Vedic Astrology Series - 1: Ashtakavarga made simple for the western astrologer. 1992

10. R.G. Krishnan. Correspondence Courses # 1, 2, 3, 4 on Vedic Astrology in English. 1992.

Glossary

Astrology
The study of the influence of the various orbiting planets on human beings and their activities. Natal Astrology deals with the effects of planetary movements on a particular individual. Mundane astrology deals with effects of planetary movements on a Nation.

Ascendant
Commonly known as the 'rising sign'. This represents the first house in any horoscope. Ascendant is determined by the time of birth in the case of Natal charts and time of the event in the case of Mundane charts.

Aspect
The angular distance between planets. For example, an angular distance of 120^0 will indicate trine aspect. In Vedic astrology aspect is considered sign wise. For example, all the planets will aspect the 7th sign reckoned from that sign.

Ayanamsa
Western astrology is based on a moveable zodiac and the Vedic Astrology is based on a fixed zodiac. The difference between the two is called Ayanamsa.

Bindu
A contributed beneficial point.

Binna AshtakaVarga
Ashtaka varga prepared for each planet separately. For example, we have Binnashtaka Varga charts for Sun, Moon, Mars, Mercury, Jupiter, Venus and Saturn.

Combust
Any planet which gets close to the Sun within a certain degree (this varies with the planet concerned) becomes combust. This means that the planet concerned becomes less powerful.

Conjunction
In Vedic Astrology conjunction is considered sign wise. Thus, two planets posited in the same sign, even if they are at different longitudes, are said to be conjunct. In Western Astrology however two planets having the same longitude are said to be conjunct.

Chart
Horoscope or chart is the map of the heavens at any point of time. This represents the planetary situation at that point of time.

Dasa
Planetary cycle. This is unique to the Vedic Astrology. The widely used dasa sytem is called 'Vimshottari dasa system'.

Dusthana
This literally means evil house. In Vedic Astrology the 6th, 8th and the 12th houses are called dusthanas.

Ephemeris
The book containing the daily longitudes of all the planets including the nodes as they move along the zodiac. This book is very useful in preparing a horoscope for a native or for any event at any point of time.

Eclipse
Eclipse is the partial or total obscurement of one celestial body. The phenomenon of Solar eclipse and Lunar eclipse occurs every year. Lunar eclipse occurs when Moon passes through the Earth's shadow. This means that Earth comes in between Sun and Moon. A Solar eclipse occurs when Moon passes between the Sun and the Earth.

Fast Moving planets
Sun, Moon, Mercury, Venus and Mars are called fast moving planets. Moon goes around the zodiac once in 27 days. Sun, Mercury and Venus take about one year and Mars takes about 18 months for going around the Zodiac.

Lunation
Lunation is the same as New Moon. This occurs once a month when Sun and Moon conjunct on the same longitude.

Lunation Chart
The horoscope prepared for any place on earth at the correct time when both Sun and Moon are conjunct on the same longitude is the Lunation chart for that place.

Karaka
Astrological significator. For example, Sun is the Karaka for father, Moon is for the mother etc.

Kalasarpa yoga
This yoga arises in any horoscope if all the planets are hemmed in between Rau and Ketu. The outer planets such as Uranus, Neptune and Pluto are not considered. This is an evil yoga and tends to nullify the good results that may accrue due to other favorable planetary situations.

Kendra
Angular houses namely 1, 4, 7 and the 10th houses from the ascenda They are also known as quadrants.

Ketu
Moon's southern node. Also called Dragon's tail.

Lagna
This is the Sanskrit name for Ascendant.

Malefic
Evil planet that causes harm.

Mutual Exchange Yoga

Mutual exchange means that two planets are mutually placed in the other's house. This is called "Parivarthana" in Sanskrit. For example, if Venus is in Aries and Mars is in Libra then there is a mutual exchange between Mars and Venus. Such mutual exchanges generally form a Rajayoga called "Parivarthana yoga".

.

Natal Chart

Horoscope of a person based on the person's date, time and place of birth.

Nakshatra

Also known as Lunar Mansion. This is a segment of the zodiac comprising of 13^0 and 20' each.There are in all 27 nakshtras covering the entire Zodiac

Navamsa

Navamsa in Sanskrit means $1/9^{th}$. Navamasa chart is evolved out of Rasi chart by dividing each sign into nine parts and placing the planets in the correct $1/9^{th}$ part. This chart is an important tools in the art of prediction.

Panchak phenomenon

This phenomenon occurs every month on a 27 days cycle. Whenever Moon transits the signs of Aquarius and Pisces and the nakshtras posited therein namely Dhanishta -3rd and the -4th padas, Satabisha- all the 4 padas, Poorvabhadrapada - all the 4padas, Uttarabhadrapada - all the 4 padas and Revathi - all the 4 padas.

Planets

The classics of Vedic Astrology refer to nine planets only namely, Sun, Moon, Mars, Mercury, Jupiter, Venus, Saturn, Rahu and Ketu. In Western astrology however, they consider in addition to the above, the three outer planets also namely, Uranus, Neptune and Pluto.

Parivarthana yoga

Please see the mutual exchange yoga as discussed above.

Trinal Houses

This is also known as 'Trikona houses". They are the 1st, 5th and the 9th houses from the ascendant or lagna.

Vedic Astrology

This is also known as 'Hindu Astrology'. Principles of Vedic Astrology were enunciated by the Great Sage Parasara about 5000 years ago.

Zodiac

The apparent path of Sun around the Earth is called Ecliptic. Zodiac is the broad band in the heavens extending for about 9^0 on either side of the Ecliptic. Zodiac is divided into 12 Zodiacal signs namely, Aries, Taurus, Cancer, Leo, Virgo, Libra, Scorpio, Sagittarius, Capricorn, Aquarius and Pisces.

Quadrant
They are the angular houses namely 1,4,7,10 houses reckoned from the ascendant. They are also called 'Kendras' in Sanskrit.

Rahu
Moon's north node. Also called Dragon's head.

Retrogression
All planets except Sun and Moon get into retrograde motion from time to time. These are given in detail in the Ephemeris. In Vedic Astrology Rahu and Ketu are always considered to be in retrograde motion.

Rishi
A sage.The great Parashara who is the father of Vedic Astrology was a Rishi.

Slow moving planets
Jupiter, Saturn, Rahu and Ketu are considered as slow moving planets in Vedic Astrology. Jupiter takes about 12 yrs, Saturn takes about 30 yrs, Rahu and Ketu take about 18 yrs to go around the zodiac. The outer planets are not considered in Vedic Astrology.

Solar Ingress Charts
These are charts prepared for the entry of Sun into the various zodiacal signs. For example, Solar ingress chart for Sun's entry into Aries will be the chart prepared for the exact time of Sun's entry into the sign of Aries.

Sidereal chart
The chart prepared by deducting the Ayanamsa from the longitudes of the planets in a Tropical chart. This is the chart as per Vedic Astrology.

Sarvashtaka Varga
This is the sum total of the binnashtaka varga of all planets. This is represented in a numerical figure in each sign. The sum total of all bindus in a Sarvashtakavarga Chart will be 337.